Outbreak and Massacre by the Dakota Indians in Minnesota in 1862:

Marion P. Satterlee's Minute Account of the Outbreak, with Exact Locations, Names of All Victims, Prisoners at Camp Release, Refugees at Fort Ridgely, etc. Complete List of Indians killed in battle and those hung, and those pardoned at Rock Island, Iowa. Interesting Items and Anecdotes

Edited by Don Heinrich Tolzmann

*Cover illustration: Defender's Monument, New Ulm, Minnesota
Courtesy of the Brown County Historical Society, New Ulm, MN*

Other Heritage Books publications by the author:

CD-ROMs:

German-American Biographical Index (CD-ROM)
The German Colonial Era (CD-ROM)
HB Archives: Germans Vol. 2 (CD-ROM)

Books:

German Pioneers in Early California: Erwin G. Gudde's History

*AMANA: William Rufus Perkins' and Barthinius L. Wick's History of
The Amana Society or Community of True Inspiration*

Pennsylvania Germans: James Owen Knauss, Jr.'s Social History

Kentucky's German Pioneers: H.A. Rattermann's History

Covington's (KY) German Heritage

*German Allied Troops in the American Revolution:
J.R. Rosengarten's Survey of German Archives and Sources*

German-Americana: A Bibliography

German Immigration in America: The First Wave

*Memories of the Battle of New Ulm: Personal Accounts of the Sioux
Uprising. L.A. Fritsche's History of Brown County, Minnesota*

Published 2001 by
HERITAGE BOOKS, INC.
1540E Pointer Ridge Place,
Bowie, Maryland 20716
1-800-398-7709 / www.heritagebooks.com

ISBN 0-7884-1896-3

Contents

Editor's Introduction

Much has been written about the 1862 Sioux Uprising, or Dakota Conflict, in Minnesota, and much more will most likely be written, as its impact was dramatic and immense.[1] An immediate result was the flight of nearly forty thousand people from their homes, and an estimated casualty count of as many as a thousand deaths.

Even today, such an event would most likely immediately command international attention and become a media event. Given the much smaller population at the time, one can readily understand what a striking impact this conflict had nationally across the U.S. in general, as well as in the state of Minnesota.

About a half a century after the event, Marion P. Satterlee of Minneapolis set out to document the Uprising, and in a number of publications tried to record the names of all those involved in the conflict, casualties, prisoners, and those executed. Due to the fact that many people were killed in the fields, in the countryside, along roadways, etc., the actual number of deaths will probably never be known.

However, on the basis of his documentation, Satterlee came up with the following statistics: a total of 490 killed (413 citizens and 77 enlisted soldiers). He also indicates that there was a total of 71 Indians who were killed, hung, or died, and that 277 were imprisoned. His documentation, therefore, provides us with essential source material dealing with the Uprising.[2]

The unique value of this work is that it not only sheds light on the 1862 Uprising that is of value for historical research, but it also amounts to a biographical index of those involved.[3]

For those seeking information on their ancestry, it is often the only place they can find information regarding the death of the ancestor. Of special value in this regard is that Satterlee also attempted to document the location of where an individual was killed.

For many years, the value of this work has been particularly recognized by descendants of those who perished during the conflict, many of them wanting to identify their ancestors, and also to locate and visit the sites where members of their families lost their lives.

However, it apparently it has not been widely known as an important documentary source, as it is rarely, if ever cited in works dealing with the Uprising. Moreover, it has been out-of-print since the 1920s.

This work originally came to my attention in the course of translating and editing works dealing with the history of <u>New Ulm, Minnesota</u>, where two battles took place during the conflict.[4]

Recognizing the importance of this work, I decided to edit it for publication, so as to make it again available and accessible to all those interested in the topic.

A special word of thanks to Darla Gebhard, Research Librarian at the Brown County Historical Society in New Ulm for all the valuable research assistance she has provided. Finally, many thanks to Dorothy Young, Germanic Languages and Literatures, University of Cincinnati, for the preparation of the manuscript.

Notes

1. For a selection of recent works dealing with the topic see: Duane Schultz, *Over the Earth I Come: The Great Sioux Uprising of 1862.* (New York: St. Martin's Press, 1992).

2.Satterlee's work originally appeared as: *A Detailed Account of the Massacre by the Dakota Indians of Minnesota in 1862.* (Marion P. Satterlee, 1925). The title on the cover of the book, however, bore the title: *Outbreak and Massacre by the Dakota Indians in 1862: A Minute Account of the Outbreak, with Exact Locations, Names of All Victims, Prisoners at Camp Release, Refugees at Fort Ridgely, etc., Complete List of Indians Killed in Battles and Those Hung, and Those Pardoned at Rock Island, Iowa, Interesting Items and Anecdotes.*

This work appears to be a compilation of earlier works by Satterlee on the topic, such as: *A Description of the Massacre by Sioux Indians in Renville County, Minnesota, August 18-19, 1862: A Complete Compilation of the Names of Victims and the Circumstances of their death so far as Known.*(Minneapolis: The Fisher Paper Box Co., 1916, and: *A Detailed Account of the Massacre by the Dakota Indians of Minnesota in 1862.* (Minneapolis: Marion P. Satterlee, 1923).

3. With regard to frontier history, see J. Norman Heard, *Handbook of the American Frontier: Four Centuries of Indian-White Relationships.* (Metuchen, New Jersey: Scarecrow Press, 1993).

4. See Don Heinrich Tolzmann, *The Sioux Uprising in Minnesota, 1862: Jacob Nix's Eyewitness History.* (Indianapolis: The Max Kade German-American Center, Indiana University-Purdue University & the Indiana German Heritage Society, 1994).

Explanatory Remarks.

Having been often asked the cause of my interest in Indian affairs, so long passed, an explanation is given. Coming to Southern Minnesota in 1863, the spring after the outbreak, my boyhood days were filled with its narratives, in which acquaintances were often participants. A daughter of Capt. Ambrose Freeman was my aunt; Wm. Everett and daughter Lily, survivors of Shetek, and Mrs. Esther Gunn, a refugee, were townsmen; and similar conditions have excited my interest continually; while writing historical sketches in newspaper work so many errors and falsifications were found that a personal investigation was determined upon. A card system was arranged for every possible victim; each name was the subject of diligent search.

Aid has been given by the Minnesota and South Dakota Historical Societies, and a personal inspection of grounds, ruins, monuments, made. To Dr. Wm. W. Folwell, Warren Upham, and Maj. R. I. Holcombe of the Minn. Society we are deeply indebted. Correspondence or interviews cover the following survivors of the outbreak:—Richard Pfefferlee, Luther Ives, Samuel McAuliff concerning Brown Co.; Wm. Wichman, Jos. Crusol, Thos. A. Robertson, Mrs. Carrothers-McNanny, Mrs. Mary E. Schwandt-Schmidt, Lewis Kitzman, Mrs. Justina Boelter, Mrs. Amelia Busse-Reynolds, Mrs. M. A. Horan, Gottlieb Reyff, John Kochendorfer, of points above Milford; Mrs. Lewis Harrington, Jesse V. Branham, A. H. Rose, Thos. Holmes, Albert H. DeLong, of McLeod, Meeker and Kandiyohi counties; Mrs. Lily Everett-Curtis of Lake Shetek; of military affairs, Maj. J. M. Bowler, A P. Connolly, George A.

Brackett. Others for information: Dan. H. Freeman, R. H. C. Hinman, Mrs. Anna Aiton-Olson, Frank Shoemaker and Miss Gratia Countryman of the Minneapolis Public Library. For translations and explanations of Indian matters, we are indebted to Samuel J. Brown and Thomas A. Robertson, both able interpreters and survivors of the outbreak. The principal aim of this work is to identify each victim, and give particulars as to location, manner and time of the death.

Without any claims to historical pre-eminence, you have the results of earnest endeavors to learn the true story of this horrible affair.

M. P. SATTERLEE.

Minneapolis, Minn., Oct. 31, 1923.

Locations—Upper side of Minnesota River from New Ulm in order going northwest: West Newton, Fort Ridgely, Magners (present Franklin), LaCroix Creek (Birch Coulie), Beaver Creek, Middle Creek, Sacred Heart Creek, Hawk Creek, Chippewa River. No one lived over three miles from the river.

On the lower side of the Minnesota Milford township was the boundary of the Reservation; just below the Agency were the bands of Wapa-xa, Wakute and Huxa-xa; the Lower Agency; just above, the bands of Big Eagle Maka-to, Traveling Hail and Little Crow; at Rice Creek two bands of Shak-pi; at the Upper Agency, various bands of Wapaton-Sissetons, who were against the outbreak from the start. With these locations in mind the reader will better follow the movements of the settlers, troops and Indians.

THE TRUE STORY

OF THE

MASSACRE BY DAKOTA INDIANS

IN MINNESOTA.

THE outrages and murders by the Dakota Indians of Minnesota, in 1862, were the culmination of the struggle between races for possession of the beautiful and prolific lands of the state, which ended in the triumph of the white man. From the establishing of Fort Snelling in 1820, the influx of white people increased in volume each year. The earliest invaders of the red man's territory were the agents and employees of the fur companies, then white hunters and trappers who took the game for their own profit; next, came the settler to the fertile soil, and building of homes and villages brought in an army of artisans. Slowly and insidiously the *until*

⁂ wiles of civilization undermined the savage race, tlil
futile opposition turned to blind rage and bloodthirsty murder. As a result the Dakotas were driv-
en from Minnesota, and stripped of their possessions.
Placed on a desolate reservation in Dakota Territory
friends and enemies of the whites were treated alike
by the government.

At the time of the outbreak the tribes were generally referred to as the Medawakantons, (people of
the lakes), or Lower Indians, which included the
Wapa-kutas (leaf shooters), living along the Minnesota River, from the township of Milford to the Yellow Medicine River, and the Sissetons, (marsh or
prairie people), or Upper Indians, who included the
Wapa-tons, (leaf people), occupied the upper portion.
An Agency for the former was established some few
miles below the mouth of the Redwood River, and
for the latter at the mouth of the Yellow Medicine
River. Thos, J. Galbraith was the Agent for both
tribes,

For 42 years the government had exerted its influence, and for 27 years the missionaries had endeavored to be the "good brother", but neither could
protect the Indian from debasement and robbery
by the whites. Whiskey was doled out to make treaties, and "boot-legged" to buy furs. Indian wrongs
were admitted, and every scalawag wanted to right
their wrongs, and usually pocket the proceeds, Indian wives, with their children, were commonly deserted and thrown back on the tribe for support, and

the disgrace and added burdens were deeply resented by individuals, the tribes and decent whites. ↴

Traders were authorized by the government, and had their trading posts on the Reservation. They did a very profitable business, for they set the prices on what the Indian had to sell, and also on what he had to buy. But extravagant business profits were not enough, so they led the Indians to make various treaties for the sale of their lands to the government; and on various pretexts secured most of the treaty money. Annuity payments were also rich harvests for the traders. ↴

In 1843 an Act of Congress was passed, providing that: *"No stipulations can be inserted in any treaty for the payment of Indian debts."* Probably a result of Traders manipulation of the treaty of 1837.

A   In 1861 Rev. S. R. Riggs wrote in public print: "One more word I say to unmarried men in this country. It is a bad place for you, that you know as well as I do. But what I want to say to you, is 'Don't keep mistresses.' If you prefer a Dakota woman, take her for good, and be faithful to her. Marriage is a matter of taste. I don't advise you to seek wives among Indians, but if that is your taste, nobody has any right to object. Only don't be mean about it; don't dishonor the community, even if it is an Indian one. Don't treasure up for yourselves, wrath against the day of wrath. Of all sins licentiousness is the most terribly ruinous of moral character, and even manhood itself. Be wise, and may God help you to shun the path of the destroyer."

B   St. Peter Tribune of June 26, 1861: "We stood around the railing, and the Indians passed in at one end, and emerged at the other. A table was placed against the door, with the gold pile upon it, and as each Indian's name was called he stepped up and took his $20 gold piece, and then came the tug of war —he had to run the gauntlet of the Traders. If he owed them anything they would take it out of his hands, whether our friend the Indian was satisfied or not. The Trader has a speedy way of collecting debts." Eleven liquor sellers were arrested by the troops at this payment.

Aside from the general abuse of the race, there were four events prominent in leading to the outbreak:— Violation of the Treaty of 1851—Indian Department mismanagement—Soldiers' Lodge—and the murders at Acton. These are treated here in justice to the Indians, and as necessary to an understanding of various phases of this affair.

THE TREATY OF 1851.

As proposed by the Indians this treaty gave for a Reservation, a ten-mile-wide strip on each side of the Minnesota River, and called for a cash payment of 10 cents per acre for all other lands. As passed by Congress, they were given only the south strip, and the President was authorized to remove them from this at his pleasure. The consideration was a cash payment of $550,000, and an annuity, which in time paid the principal. Much of this was diverted to school and other purposes repugnant to the Indians. But they had to accept. When the Indians signed the treaty they were subjected to a gross fraud right in presence of the Agent, Treaty Officials and supposed friends including the Missionaries. In the same room, and on a table adjoining the one on which the Treaty was signed, was the "Traders' Paper", which was an order on the Agent to pay to the Traders alleged claims against the tribes for the sum of $431,735.78. Some claims dated back to 1837, none were verified, and the list was not completed, nor attached when signed. It was an evasion of law and a dishonest collection of unproven claims.

To this second paper, these savages who could neither read nor write, were led and caused to "touch the pen", held by a white man. When the Indians learned, some weeks later, what the paper meant, they went to Agent Ramsey and he promised them that he would disregard the "Traders Paper" but later he paid most of the money to one Hugh Tyler, an agent for the Traders. The finale of the matter was, that outside a few who were helping to defraud their brothers, and nine chiefs who were bribed, no Indian received any money. Hugh Tyler collected $55,000 for his services; Agent Ramsey kept $25,000 as he alleged at his trial in the matter before Congress, for expenses of removing the Indians to the reservation—any record of expending or returning it is not found. Wapa-sha's bribe money was taken by Franklin Steele. and he testified under oath, that he had never received any of it. This bribery and all sorts of "influence" was used to secure a receipt from the Indians to satisfy the government, without surrendering the money. Ramsey imprisoned Chief Red Iron, "Maza-sha" and tried to take away his chieftainship because he would not sign, and had advised others to "let Ramsey send the money back, as he theatened to do". *a*

A How beautifully the Ordinance of 1787 reads: "The utmost good faith shall always be observed toward the Indians; their lands and property shall never be taken from them without their consent, and in their property rights and liberty they never shall be invaded or disturbed, unless in just and lawful wars authorized by Congress; but laws founded in justice and humanity shall from time to time be made for preventing wrongs being done to them and preserving peace and friendship with them".—1 Stat. 50.

Despite this treatment Red Iron was faithful to the whites in the massacre. It was distinctly agreed in the treaty that, "The money shall be paid to the chiefs, in open council as they shall determine", but this too was avoided. Though the committee found that Ramsey "Was not authorized by any law to recognize the Traders Paper", nothing was done, and restitution was not made by the government, but the land was put on sale at $1.25 per acre; more than 400 per cent profit. It was not difficult to enrage people who had been so outraged. A remark of Little Crow, when pressed to join in the outbreak, was: "Maybe we can get our land back, and sell it to them (the whites) again".

INDIAN DEPARTMENT MIS-MANAGEMENT.

Inkpa-duta, (Scarlet Point), was the leader of a small band of renegade Indians, mostly Wapa-kutas, who had long been separated from the tribes on account of their misbehavior and general character. These miscreants committed the massacre at Spirit Lake in 1857. Soldiers failed to find this band, and later the Department demanded that the others go out and capture or kill these marauders, and actually held up the annuity money due the innocent people until they attempted to comply, and did kill one, a son of Inkpa-duta. This injustice had two results on the Indians—they recognized the wrong, and set soldiers down as incompetent or cowardly. When the messengers came back and reported the murders at Acton, it was at once surmised that guilty and innocent would suffer alike. The conclusion was that they "might as well die fighting as to be starved to death by the Whites".

Attempt was made to force merchandise on the Indians in place of money due them.

They were offered paper money in place of gold specified by the treaty. As they knew nothing of the value of paper money, it was refused.

Agent Galbraith was a political appointee, unacquainted with Indians, or their government; he held office but a short time before the outbreak. The annuity money for 1862 was due in June, and arrived at Fort Ridgely on August 18th. The Indians said that Robert was at St. Paul, trying to hold out the Traders' claims. He was with the money when it reached the fort.

Late in July the Sisseton bands came down from their homes on the prairies, to the Upper Agency, for their annuity. They were in a destitute condition, and several died from hunger and exposure. Despite the fact, that there was food in the warehouse designed for these bands Galbraith refused to issue it. On the 4th of August matters became desperate and the Indians broke into the warehouse and took some of the supplies by force. Lieut. Timothy Sheehan's company of soldiers stopped the looting and a council was agreed upon to adjust matters. Capt. John S. Marsh, in command at Fort Ridgely was sent for. Galbraith issued the supplies and the Sissetons went home for the buffalo hunt. Matters were even worse at the Lower Agency, and it was promised to issue food there. This Galbraith failed to do, but set about organizing a mixed-blood company for service in the south. This promise was evidently an important event, and is the first subject mentioned when Sibley opened communication with Little Crow after the Birch Coulie battle.

Another matter has been shown in a book published by a Mrs. Barton, the daughter of Rev. John P. Williamson the missionary at the Lower Agency. She relates that a council was held, shortly before the massacre, at which the Traders were present. That after some parley by Galbraith with the Traders, in regard to giving the Indians credit, Little Crow said; "When men are hungry, they find a way to get what they want." There was a dead silence; the aged interpreter Philander Prescott, knowing the seriousness of the situation, hesitated to make the interpretation. Galbraith then asked Williamson to tell him, which he did. Galbraith then demanded of the Traders: "What are you going to do?" at which they got up and went aside for consultation. They shortly came back and sat down in silence, when the Agent again demanded their conclusions. Andrew Myrick said; "So far as I am concerned, they can eat grass or their own dung," and he walked away. There was a wild uproar, and the council broke up in confusion, amid Indian yells and white men's curses. On the morning of the 18th, Ta-wasu-ota (His many hails) killed James Lynd, clerk for Myrick, saying: "Now, I will kill the dog who would not give me credit", and Myrick was killed and his mouth was stuffed with grass, as if in Indian retaliation.   Little Crow, in his letter to Gen. Sibley after the battle at Birch Coulie, makes statements confirming the fact of such a council.

THE SOLDIERS' LODGE.

As the Traders were "always at the 'pay table' " the Indians determined not to be robbed of their annuity money and formed a Soldiers' Lodge.   A lodge is organized when any occasion calls for united action and direction of affairs is necessary,   The braves become members and select a leader who "leads the warpath", or carries out the wishes of the lodge.   In such an organization orders are imperative and must be obeyed under penalty.   Being thus organized, the Lower Indians did most of the bloody work, until demoralized by liquor and over-eating.   Had they observed the same unity of action, as at the Agency, the Minnesota valley would have been cleared of the white people.

The Traders learning of the formation of a lodge at once resented it, by refusing credit, and resorting to personal abuse and threats.   Thus an organization already inflamed against the white people was ready to act.   But liquor from the warehouses and private homes was obtained, and pursuant to Indian custom, immediately made use of, so that even the Soldiers' Lodge was helpless.   Between horse-stealing, drunkenness and over-eating, they failed to act: Ridgely was re-inforced, New Ulm was occupied and barricaded, and troops were coming to the rescue. The fighting was weak and indifferent, and many were trying to avoid participation.

MURDERS AT ACTON.

The murder of five persons, on Sunday Aug. 18, was simply the opening point for the outbreak. We have shown the outrageous treatment of the Indians, and in particular the Inkpa-duta incident where the annuity money was held up. Now, they had only a small hunting ground, and that shared with white hunters, better equipped than they were, so their very living depended on their justly earned annuity, now long over due. There are but two motives for these murders: A hatred of the whites for their injustice, or as a result of the quarrel with Jones, or possibly of both. When the murders became known fear of white injustice was immediate, and a determination to refuse to surrender the guilty ones, by their friends, made a near war certain, and taunts of cowardice won many to decide with Little Crow, to "fight and die like brave Dakotas." Beyond doubt the previous fraud and compulsion made the massacre possible. Jones had sold Indians whiskey, and was one who had no respect for Indians, or for their rights. He was abusive and domineering, and it is probable that the immediate Acton affair was an outburst of passion, which was capitalized by a long line of abuse preceding it.

Acton township postoffice, the home of Robinson

Jones, was situated about ten miles west of present Litchfield, and three miles southeast of present Atwater. A party of about 20 Indians, of whom Island Cloud "Marpiya-witak" was the head-man, were on a hunting trip; six of whom came to Jones' place. One of them had borrowed a gun from Jones, and he had failed to return it. An angry altercation ensued and the Indians sullenly left, going toward the home of Howard Baker, a son of Mrs. Jones, (Mrs. Ann Baker), by a former marriage. Jones' took his gun and followed them, accompanied by his wife. Clara D. Wilson a young girl, and an 18 months old boy, both relatives, were left in the house, with the doors locked. Arriving at Bakers' shortly after the Indians had come, the quarrel was renewed, but soon dropped and a trade for a gun was made between Baker and one of the Indians. Then on a banter, all the men, (except Viranus Webster, who accompanied by his wife, was stopping at Bakers while seeking a location) joined in a shooting contest. None of the white men reloaded, but the Indians did. Arriving at the house Jones stepped around the corner to reload his gun, when suddenly the Indians shot and killed Howard Baker, standing in the door, Mrs. Jones sitting just inside, and Viranus Webster who was bringing some needed articles from his wagon. Mrs. Webster, who was in the wagon, was not molested; Mrs. Baker fell

A. Jones must have been in poor repute with his neigbors, from tales of the settlers. He had been married to Mrs. Ann Baker some nine months, but she is buried at Ness cemetery under the name of Ann Baker, and a monument erected by the state.

or jumped into the cellar with her baby in her arms, and her young son lying on the bed was unharmed. Jones started to run to the brush near by and was shot down, dying in terrible agony about an hour after. The Indians left and going back past Jones' house, shot through a pantry window killing Clara Wilson. They did not enter either house, molest the property or mutilate the dead. The women after the Indians left tried to assist Jones; soon as he died they took the two children and fled to a neighbors' and gave the alarm. Settlers were notified, and an an inquest was held next day, August 18th, and the bodies were prepared for burial. As the party was starting for the Ness Settlement cemetery some distance away, 11 Indians appeared and the settlers endeavored to approach them, but they evidently apprehended danger and fled. The Indians who committed the murders stole a team from A. M. Ecklund, with which they returned home, and told of their bloody deeds.

When this band resolved to stand by the men involved, the whole band proceeded to the camp of Little Crow some miles down the river. He was awakened and a demand made that he "lead the warpath" against the Whites. It is said that he refused, and that so powerfully was he moved by the situation, that great beads of perspiration stood out on his face. He had been across the states to Washington and knew how hopeless a war would be; but he realized that his people were going to war, with or without him, and that refusal would brand him as a coward among them, and white people would not respect him more. When he consented, it was with the full realization that he was a doomed man. He said he would do his best, and die fighting; this promise he kept. After being shot through the body he endeavored to kill his enemy.

A council was held and plans laid for an attack on the Agency at daybreak. When all was ready most of the bands started for the Agency, picking up the bands of Good Thunder, "Wakinyan-washta", White Dog, "Shonka-ska", and Big Eagle, "Wamditanka", whose villages lay on their way. They arrived at Robert's store about 6:30 a. m.

MASSACRE AT THE
REDWOOD OR LOWER AGENCY.

The Agency was located on the high bank of the Minnesota river, about two miles below the present town of Morton. Agent, employee, and other buildings were ranged about an open space called Council Square, and the Traders' were along the river above; Robert's the most distant being a half-mile away. A road from the ferry crossed the river bottom some half mile, joining the roads to Fort Ridgely, another road passed through the Agency grounds following down the river to New Ulm. On this road a mile or more below were the villages of Wapa-sha, (Red Leaf), Wa-kuta, (Leaf Shooter), and Hu-sha-sha, (Red Legs), who were called by messenger, but not believing, or realizing the situation, they were late at Agency murders. With true Indian sagacity, small parties gathered at each store, and waited for the signal. Ta-wasu-ota was seen to run from Robert's to Myrick's store, where James Lynd stood in the doorway, and shouting "Now, I will kill the dog who would not give me credit", shot and killed him. At once the shooting began. Geo. W. Divoll was next; Andrew Myrick ran up the stairs. The Indians being afraid to follow, proposed to burn the building; he dropped out of a back window and ran toward the river, but was killed.   Myrick's cook, known on- as "Old Fritz," was the next victim.

Francois LaBathe was killed in his store, which was near Myrick's.   At Forbes' store Geo. W. Spen- cer and Wm. Bourrat, clerks, ran upstairs, Spencer was severely wounded; Wakinyan-tawa, (His Thun- der), appeared and saved Spencer, who was found at Camp Release.   Bourratt endeavored to escape from the rear, but was shot down at the edge of the bluff.   He feigned death, and the Indians threw a log on him and left.   He crawled away and despite the wound through his groin, traveled to a point near St. Cloud, and recovered.   At the Robert store they killed Patrick McClellan, Joseph Belland and Antoine Young.

The state of affairs at the stores was soon dis- covered at the Agency grounds and the people fled, mostly to the ferry, but some down the New Ulm road.   Indians came to the barns at the edge of the bluff, and killed A. H. Wagner, Supt. of Farms, John Lamb and Lathrop Dickinson his assistants, and took the horses.   Interpreter Philander Prescott was warned to "stay in his house" but fearing he would not be safe, even with his Indian wife and their child- ren, he fled but was killed.   It is said that Shak-pe (Little-six), killed him.   Agency Physician, Philander P. Humphrey, appointed in the previous May, fled with his sick wife, and three children, and reached

Edward Magner's place, some four miles below.   The
wife being exhausted they entered the house, and the
oldest boy, John A., was sent to a nearby spring for
water.   Indians came and killed Humphrey outside
and when the wife barred the door, the wretches
set fire to the house burning her and the two children to death.   John witnessed the affair, from the
brush and then fled to the fort.   Alexander Hunter,
a cripple from frozen feet, fled with his young wife,
(a mixed-blood nee Marian Robertson), on the New
Ulm road, but were induced by Indian friends to stop
at one of the villages, over night.   Tuesday morning
they had gone but a short ways when they were captured.   Hinhan-shoon-koyag-mani, (Walks clothed
in an owls tail), shot and killed Hunter, and claimed
the woman as his captive.   She was rescued at Camp
Release.   Her father was Andrew Robertson a Supt.
of Indian Schools [died, 1859].   A brother Frank escaped from the Prescott home, but was taken prisoner at Beaver Creek.   Two brothers, named Martelle, owned the ferry, which was operated by Jacob
Mauley, (his proper name was Hubert Millier).   He
remained all through the shooting and flight, and was
probably waiting for any other fugitives when killed,
at his post of duty.   It is a disgrace to the State of
Minnesota that this brave Frenchman, who saved at
least 37 people from the massacre, has never been
recognized publicly.   Peter Martelle was killed near
the stone mound at Morton, Oliver and wife reached
the fort.   Rev. S. D. Hinman, Episcopal minister,

and an assistant Emily J. West, escaped to the fort; Mrs. Hinman and children were away visiting at Faribault at the time. J. W. DeCamp was away, and his wife and three children, were saved by Wa-kuta, though they were made prisoners. Later on they were aided to escape from the hostiles by Towan-iteton, (Face of the village, baptized as Lorenzo Lawrence), and taken to Fort Ridgely. They learned at the fort that the husband and father had been killed at the Birch Coulie battle.

George Gleason, Galbraith's clerk, was returning from the Upper Agency, accompanied by the wife of Dr. J. B. Wakefield, Upper Agency physician, and two children. Near the Redwood river they met two Indians, named only as Chaska and Hepan, (first and second born sons), who killed Gleason and took the others to the hostile camp. Both these Indians were hanged at Mankato, though Mrs. Wakefield declares Chaska innocent of the murder, and says he saved her life and others. In a pamphlet she published she says she was told that he was not among those to be hung. He was listed as Chaska-dan or Chaska-ite, (Little, or Face of, first-born son). There may be merit in her claims; at least one Indian, half-witted, was hung for being present at the murder of Amos Huggins; the trials were pretty informal and most people not very particular.

It is remarkable that no detailed account worth consideration, by any of those present, except that of Rev. Hinman, has been recorded. Several have

given partial accounts describing their personal ex-
periences only. Hinman lived on the right of the
Council Square, opposite the government warehouse.
Beside him, toward the river was Prescott, and beyond him Dickinson's boarding house. On the opposite side the warehouse, Dr. Humphrey, employe
lodging house, and barns at the edge of the bluff.

He says, in the Heard history:

"I arose early expecting to go to Faribault; had just
finished breakfast, and was sitting outside smoking a
pipe and talking with a mason about a job which he had
just finished, upon the new church which I was building. Presently I saw a number of Indians passing
down, nearly naked, and armed with guns. The mason exclaimed: "I guess they are going to have a
dance". "No," said Dr. Humphrey's son, who was
standing near us, "They have guns, and are not going
to dance". Then I noticed that instead of going by,
they commenced sitting down on the steps of various
buildings. About this time I heard the guns in the upper town. A man by the name of Whipple said, "He
guessed the Chippewa had come over and they were
having a battle." He then crossed the road to his
boarding house. I soon noticed that the people at the
boarding house, who could see the upper stores, were
running down the bluff. Then four Indians came down
the street. One of them left the others and went into
the Indian farmer Prescott's house, and came immediately out. Frank Robertson a young clerk in the em-
ploy of the government, followed him out, looking very
pale. I asked him what was the matter. He said he
didn't know, but that the Indian told them all to stay
in the house. He told me he thought there was going
to be trouble, and started for Beaver Creek, a few miles

above, where his mother lived. Soon White Dog form-
erly president of the farmer Indians, ran past very
much frightened. I asked him what the matterwas and
he said that there was awful work, and that he was
going to see Wapa-sha about it. Then Crow, in company with another Indian, went by the gate, and I asked
Crow what was the matter. He was usually very po-
lite, but now he made no answer, and, regarding me
with a savage look, went on toward the stable the next
building below. Just before, Wagner ran by, and I
asked him also what the trouble was. He said the Indians were going to the stable to steal horses, and that
he was going there to stop them. I told him he had better not, as I was afraid there was trouble. He paid no
attention to what I said. The next I saw was the Indians leading away the horses and Wagner, Lamb and
another person trying to prevent them. By this time
Crow had reached them, and I heard him say to the Indians: "What are you doing? Why don't you shoot
these men? What are you waiting for?" Immediately
the Indians fired, wounding Wagner, who escaped
across the river to die, and killing Lamb and the other
man."\ɑ

All the buildings were looted and burned, with
the exception of Myrick's cook-house. This and the
blackened stone walls of the warehouse and church
were mute evidences of the horrible work of the sav-

A As Mr. Hinman was away from the barns, at least 600 feet, some doubt
as to Little Crow's orders is permissible. This is the only murder which can
be traced to him. Another account says that an employe drove a pitchfork
into one of the Indians, and the shooting followed. By the aid of Samuel J.
Brown and E. B. Haney, (who buried the body), we have found that Lathrop
Dickinson was killed at this time and place, and his head cut off, and thrown
on the manure heap. Probably he was the one who used the fork, and mutila-
tion was the Indian resentment. Dickinson was a brother of J. C. who kept the
boarding house, yet no history mentions his name.

age hands. Nothing alive was there when night fell, and the dead bodies laid where they were, until buried by Maj. Brown's party on Sept. 1st.

AMBUSH AT THE REDWOOD FERRY.

Capt. John S. Marsh, in command at Fort Ridgely was warned of the trouble at the Agency, at about 10 o'clock, by the refugees. He immediately sent a recall for Company C, 5th Regt., under Lieut. Timothy Sheehan, which had left that morning for Fort Ripley. He also sent J. C. Dickinson to St. Peter for Agent Galbraith, and re-inforcements. It was probably about noon when he started for the Agency with some 40 men of his Co. C, 5th Regt. He saw several of the murdered, and was warned by Hinman and others of his inadequate force to deal with the situation, but deemed it his duty to go on. He dismounted those who were in wagons, and without advance guards marched right up to the ferry in close formaiton. Only one Indian, Shonka-ska "White Dog", was in sight, on the opposite bank. There is much disagreement as to what he said, but of a sudden Interpreter Peter Quinn cried "Look out!", and immediately the Indians opened fire from the opposite bank, and from the brush just above the troops. Quinn was pierced by a dozen bullets, and some 20 of the men fell at the same time. The fire was immediately returned by the few not disabled. It was the intention of the Indians to cut the ferry ropes and shoot the soldiers while the boat was helpless in

the stream. Benedict Juni a boy prisoner says that
Indians were shooting at tin pans floating in the
river during the day.   Capt. Marsh led his small
squad down the river through the underbrush, some
distance, when it was deemed best to cross.   In the
endeavor to do so Capt. Marsh was siezed with
cramps and drowned.   The rest continued down the
river, and reached the fort late at night.   The dead
were: Capt. Marsh, Interpreter Quinn, Sergeants
Solon A. Trescott, and R. H. Findley, Corp. Joseph
S. Besse, John Holmes, Christian Joerger, James H.
Kerr, Henry McAllister, John W. Parks, John Parsley, Nathaniel Pitcher, Henry A. Shephard, Nathan
Stewart, Chas. R. Bell, Edwin F. Cole, Charles E.
French, John Gardner, Jacob A. Gehring, Darius
Kanzig, Wendell Kusda, Wenzell Norton, Moses P.
Parks, Harrison A. Phillips and Chas. W. Smith.

Monuments or markers are placed for Wapa-sha
village, at the north ferry landing, the Agency and
trading houses, and Little Crow village.

Only one Indian, To-wa-to (All blue), was killed
and a few wounded.   The effect of the successful
encounter on the Indians was indescribable.   They
proclaimed that they could "Drive the Whites out
with clubs, and would soon have their land back."
The doubting were convinced, the halting driven into line; the Soldiers Lodge issued imperative orders
to discard white men's clothing, don the breech-clout
and move into the hostile camp, and the order was
obeyed of necessity and ·forthwith.   That night all

encamped at Little Crow's village some three miles up the river.   Here were assembled the jubilant half-drunk braves, the motley-arrayed squaws and children (in the plunder), weeping and wounded captives. Trouble and dissension started among the captors, over the prisoners.   It was understood that all the Whites were to be killed, yet every raiding party had brought in women and children, and resolutely defended them.   Wapa-sha, Wa-kuta and many others who surmised a failure of the outbreak, joined in the protection.   Death was many times threatened, but records show only a child, Gustave Kittman, murdered in the hostile camp during the six weeks captivity.   Many of the captives were kept in Little Crow's house, (built by the government).   Others were in the tipis, and were often concealed and protected from the vicious braves.   Four persons were aided to escape from this camp, one by Little Crow personally.

MASSACRES IN THE SETTLEMENTS.

MURDERS AT BEAVER CREEK.

Beaver Creek, is some six miles above the present Morton, and was a settlement having a number of good horses. These were the object of a party which from settlers tales must have come there while the Agency massacre was in progress, or even before. The desire of an Indian to own a horse, saved several persons during the outbreak, as will be shown. The first alarm was Indians trying to catch settler's animals pastured in the river bottoms. The settlers were warned that there was serious trouble by Thos. A. Robertson, a mixed-blood, and told they had best get away. Soon the families of N. D. White, S. R. Henderson, David and James Carrothers, and an employe Jehiel Wedge gathered at the home of J. W. Earle, (White and James Carrothers being absent), with what teams they could gather. They started across the prairie for the fort, but had scarcely gone 40 rods when surrounded by Indians who demanded the teams and wagons. Being almost defenseless they hoped to escape by complying. After a parley, it was agreed to give up all but the wagon containing

Mrs. Henderson lying sick in bed.   Then this was demanded; the horses were surrendered and they started on, pulling the wagon by hand, following those on foot.   Suddenly the Indians opened fire.   Hoping to parley further Henderson and Wedge held up a white flag, which was not respected; Wedge was killed and Henderson's fingers shot off.   Seeing that resistance was impossible, and that the women and children could not escape, it was decided that each care for themselves.   The women and younger children were taken prisoner;   the bed with Mrs. Henderson on it, was pulled to the ground and set fire.   One infant was beaten to death over the wagon wheel and then thrown on the fire; the other was cut up and thrown on piecemeal.   Henderson was killed later at Birch Coulie, completing the extinction of this family.

Mr. Earle, who was quite corpulent, was becoming exhausted in the chase, when his son Radnor, 15 years old, with his gun loaded only with a pebble, faced the Indians, and lying down in the grass, kept them at bay till his father had gotten some distance. As soon as he fired his gun, two Indians who flanked him, shot him to death. The father was saved by his noble act. Willie and Johnnie, little sons of David Carrothers, and Eugene White, 16 years old, were also killed. The rest escaped by separating and hiding in the grass and marshes. Those escaping were: J. W. Earle, and sons Chalon A., Ezmon W., and Herman E.; S. R. Henderson, David Carrothers, and Millard W. White. Taken as prisoners were: Mrs.

Earle, daughters Julia and Elmira, Mrs. James Carrothers and two infant children, Mrs. David Carrothers and infant, Mrs. White, daughter Julia and baby Frank. All were taken to Little Crow's village, across the river. Mrs. James Carrothers, only 19 years old, was permitted to escape with her two babies, and after eight days of terrific hardship they reached Fort Ridgely utterly exhausted. Despite all this she lived to the age of 78, dying at Dodge Center in 1920. The other prisoners were at Camp Release, and were surrendered to Gen. Sibley. The Renville County Pioneers have erected monuments at the spot where Mrs. Henderson was killed, and at the place where Radnor Earle fell. a

D. Wichman, F. W. Schmidt, Henry Ahrens and some others, living on Sections 14 and 15 made their escape through the efforts of Mr. Wichman. He was employed at the Agency, and was waiting to ferry over when the flight commenced. He ran all the way to his home, warned his neighbors, and with them, fled on the bluff road to Fort Ridgely.

Near the mouth of Beaver Creek, on Secs. 25-26 and 35-36 lived Benedict Juni, Sr., Patrick and John Hayden, John Zimmermann and Balthasar Eisenreich families. When the alarm was given Zimmer-

A In her narrative, Mrs. Carrothers mentions a "medicine man" whose hatred of the Hendersons led to the atrocities, but whose friendship for herself saved the others. Though she knew him well, and spoke the Dakota fluently, she never mentions his name. We have reason to believe that he was Cetan-Honka, (Parent hawk), who was hung at Mankato. Her reason for silence is obvious if this is correct.

man, his wife (who was blind), three sons and two daughters, Mrs. Juni and five children, Mrs. Hayden and baby, started for the fort on the river road. At LaCroix Creek, opposite the Agency, they were attacked, and Zimmermann and sons John and Gottlieb were killed. Mrs. Hayden, with her babe in her arms, jumped into the brush and escaped to the fort. The rest of the party were taken to the deserted Faribault house, nearby. Suddenly the Indians left; on account probably of the approach of Marsh's men and they made their way to the fort. Of those who remained to care for the stock, Juni escaped to the fort, but Benedict, Jr. was captured, and at Camp Release. The Haydens started for the fort with the Eisenreich family, and had gone a short way, when the three men were killed, and Mrs. Eisenreich an her four children were captured.

IN MIDDLE CREEK TOWNSHIP.

On Sec. 7, lived John Zitloff, a widower, with his son and wife Mary (nee Juni), and near them three sons-in-law, John J. Meyer, William Inefeldt, an John Seig, also Louis Thiele. On their way to the Agency Michael Zitloff, Mrs. Inefeldt and Lena Juni near Beaver Creek, saw some Indians with Henderson's team, and heard much shooting at the Agency. Apprehending trouble Zitloff turned back, and Len Juni went to her parents. Mrs. Inefeldt told her husband of the circumstances, and he sent her to Meyers' saying he would follow. She went back to see what kept him and found him dead on the floor. She ran back to Meyers' where all were waiting to start. There were in the party: John Zitloff, Michael Zitloff and wife, Mrs. Inefeldt and child, John Sieg, wife and three children, John J. Meyer, wife and three children, Ernest Hauf and his two little girls, who had come from some little distance to the west; (his wife and two other children had been murdered at the home), and Louis Thiele, wife and child.

The party had driven only few rods, when the Indians rose up from a corn-field and attacked them, killing all but Thiele, Meyer, Mrs. Inefeldt and child and Mrs. Michael Zitloff. The men escaped in the underbrush. A few minutes later Mrs. Zitloff was shot and killed. Hauf, taking a child under each arm, started to run, but was shot down and his girls were kicked to death, ending this family. Zitloff is usually given as "Sitzton" in the meagre and incomplete accounts.

The settlement on Sections 33, 34 and 35, Flora twp., were veritable slaughter fields, 39 people being killed there. Johann Schwandt, living on the S. W. ¼ Sec. 33, was shingling his house when shot, and the body fell to the ground These were also killed: the wife, and sons Frederick 7, and Christian 5 years old, John Walz and wife Caroline (nee Schwandt), a son of a neighbor, John Frass. August, 11 years old, ran to the brush and reached the fort. A daughter Mary E., was captured near Fort Ridgely, as will be related. A monument marks this home.

The home of John Kochendorfer, some 80 rods away, was attacked and Kochendorfer was shot down in the dooryard, and the baby Sarah and the wife, in the house. The father lived long enough to direct his other three children to hide in the brush; they escaped to the fort, aided by Michael Boelter and the Ernest Lenz family.

Eusebius Reyff, on the S. E. ¼ of Sec. 35, was getting up hay, and was in his barnyard with a load, when he and his son Benjamin were killed. The wife and daughter Annie were killed in the dooryard. A daughter Mary, and son Emanuel were absent at the time.

John Roessler on N. E. ¼ of Sec. 34, with his wife, were grinding a scythe when the savages approached and killed them; two children were killed and thrown on as ash pile. Frederick Roessler, probably related, was killed, but no record. but that of the Evangelical Church, a mere statement is found.

Michael Boelter, on the S. W. ¼ of 35 was joined by his brother John on the S. E. ¼ of 34, and with them lived their father Gottlieb and wife. On the morning of the 18th, Michael and Emiel Grundman and August Frass, who lived beyond at Sacred Heart, were on the way to the Agency for supplies at about 11 o'clock, when they discovered the bodies of a woman and two children, evidently killed by Indians. (Mrs. Ernest Hauf and children.) They visited several homes finding only the dead; they then hurried to their homes with the awful news. Reaching home, Michael found his mother and his three children murdered and mutilated, at the house. On calling to the field where his wife, father and brother had been at work, he was answered by Indian yells, and beat a hasty retreat. These three were killed in the field, and it is likely that John Boelter is the man who bit the thumb of Cut Nose nearly off in a death struggle. Michael had warned John's wife, Justina, of danger, and running to the house, he picked up the baby boy Julius, and told Justina to follow him. She took the other two children and started, but hearing the Indians coming, hid in the underbrush and they passed by her. For nearly nine weeks they stayed in this hiding place living on herbs and some raw vegetables from the field. One of the children Emilia, died from exposure and hunger, in the fourth week. The poor woman was terribly frightened by the shooting about her; first by Indians then by the searching parties; she undoubtedly heard the battle at Birch Coulie, and for several days the hostile camp was just across the Minnesota river. She finally resolved to die in her own home and managed to reach it with the remaining child, and was there when discovered by two soldiers of a searching party. This on Monday, just nine weeks from the day she left it. The condition of the woman and child was so pitiful that the soldiers were moved to tears. Her history is remarkable. Later she married her brother-in-law Michael, by whom she bore several children; she was alive and in a fair mental condition as late as 1919.

At Gottfried Busse's, (N. W. ¼, Sec. 35,) a son, August was sent to John Roessler's on an errand and found all murdered, as described. The family fled to the cornfield, but later attempted to reach the woods when the Indians discovered them and shot to death Busse, the wife, Bertha and Caroline, infants, which the parents carried in their arms. August, Wilhelmina and Amelia were prisoners at Camp Release. Wilhelmina, (Minnie Buce-Carrigan), wrote an interesting account of her captivity, and her companions. She died in 1909. At about 18 years of age, August determined to revenge himself on the Indians. It is believed that he perished with Custer's command in the Big Horn battle.

At the home of John Lettou, (N· E. ¼, Sec. 1, Delhi Twp.), Rev. Christian L. Seder was a guest. He had conducted services alternately at the Middle Creek and Sacred Heart settlements on Sundays, for the German Evangelical Church, and the gathering at Lettou's the 17th had been a large one. Word of the trouble came, and he remained to aid in the preparations for flight. When leaving, he led the way, but a short distance off was shot and killed; Lettou and a small son were killed, but the mother and four children escaped to Fort Ridgely.

Gottlieb Manweiler, (on N. W. ¼, Sec. 1, Delhi Twp.), was a son-in-law of Ernest Lenz. He was making ready to go, when Indians appeared and he was killed. His wife, and sister, Augusta Lenz were approaching, from the Lenz home, and just came in in sight. They turned and ran back, but Augusta was overtaken and captured. Manweiler was Supt. of the Middle Creek sunday school.

The William Schmidt family, (S. E. $\frac{1}{4}$, Sec. 2, Delhi Twp.), had started to leave, but stopped for feed for the team, when Indians attacked them and killed both parents and two children, and left five-year old Minnie for dead. She revived, and later August Schwandt, in his flight, found and carried her some distance, when he became exhausted, and left her at deserted house, promising to send help. The Indians came soon and took her to the hostile camp. She was tenderly cared for by women prisoners, but died at Fort Ridgely shortly after the rescue. This completed the murder of this family.

The massacre of the Sacred Heart settlers has been mentioned but partially. The following story from obtainable accounts, personal information, and some assumptions, is as near as can be obtained, and is the only detailed account published. The settlement was near Sacred Heart Creek, and was known by that name, though the most of the people lived in Flora Twp. Paul Kitzman had the S. W. $\frac{1}{4}$, his brother-in-law Frederick Krieger the S. E. $\frac{1}{4}$, Michael Yess the N. W. $\frac{1}{4}$, of Sec. 18, William Lammers the N. E., Emiel Grundman the S. W., August Frass the S. E. $\frac{1}{4}$, of Sec. 19. The massacre was on N. W. $\frac{1}{4}$, of Sec. 20. Other families lived near, but but locations are not identified. Boelter, Frass and Grundman spread the alarm as previously stated,

and it was decided to meet at Kitzman's and start to
the fort.   Meantime, messengers sent to Schwandt's
returned with news of the murders there.   At about
8 o'clock that evening, 13 families, with 11 teams,
drove a distance on the fort road, and then keeping
to the northeast, toward present Renville; as the
teams were mostly oxen, and there were no roads,
they had made about 14 miles by next morning.   A
party of Indians, eight in number, came up and in-
quired where they were going, and being informed of
the murders, declared that the Chippewas had done
this, and they were hunting them, to kill them.   It
seems that Kitzman knew some of them, and was
led to believe their stories, so the party turned back
toward their homes under escort of the Indians who
soon began to act suspiciously.   The settlers were
poorly armed, and feared to attempt resistance, so
plodded on.   When in sight of the settlement, the
Indians fired on them, killing all but three of the
men.   They were soon shot down, and women and
children beaten and tomahawked to death.   Details
by families follow:

Kitzman Family—Paul, wife, infant Paul, Pauline and Wilhelmina, killed.   Captured: Louis and
Gustave.   The latter a child of three years, was cut
to pieces by Indians, because he cried so much.

Krieger Family—Killed, Frederick, and infant
son.   Captured, Henrietta, 5 years old.   Escaped:
John, Gottlieb and Lizzie Lehn, his step-children;
Tillie, Caroline and Minnie, his own children, and

Justina the wife.   Henrietta was captured and was at Camp Release, and the fate of a baby boy is unknown.   Justina was wounded with buckshot, and her clothes stripped from her, but later revived and clothing herself at their home, started for the fort. Wandering about in a dazed condition, she was rescued by Capt. Grant's company, but lay in a wagon during the entire Birch Coulie battle unscathed.   In nearly all histories, her thrilling story is found.   Later she married John J. Meyer, whose family were all killed at Zitloff's.

August Frass, was killed; his wife, and two children were rescued at Camp Release.   John, an older son was killed at Schwandt's place.

Emiel Grundman, wife, and two children were killed.   One little daughter had one hand shot off, and was with a younger brother, two children of Horning, two of Thiel (or Tille), two of Krieger, Mrs. Anna Zabel, left for dead but later revived. These and some others who had escaped to the woods gathered at the Krieger home, but later, becoming alarmed some ran to the woods, leaving the younger, and the badly wounded children behind.   Indians came and burned the house, and with it, either dead or alive, seven children.

August Horning and wife were killed outright, and two sons, aged 1 and 2 years old were burned in the Krieger house on the 20th.

John Urban was harvesting near New Ulm, at this time.   Mrs. Urban and children Ernestine, Rose,

Louise and Albert were captured and were rescued at Camp Release. A son August escaped with those who were at the Krieger home, to the fort.

Gottlieb Zable was killed, but the wife escaped, to the fort as described.

John (?) Neuman was with Urban at New Ulm. Mrs. Neuman and three children were taken to the hostile camp. But before the battle at Wood Lake, Ana-wang-mani (hobbles walking), a christian Wapa-ton, took them from the camp to the fort, at the risk of his own life.

T. Krause was mounted on horseback, and just before the massacre determined to go to the fort for help. He left the others and rode off, but evidently had to desert the horse, for Indians had it next morning, but he reached the fort. Mrs. Krause and two children, and a sister-in-law Pauline Krause were at Camp Release.

William Lammers was killed, the wife and two children were at Camp Release.

Michael Yess was away from home. Mrs. Yess was caught in the trace chains of an ox team which ran into the brush; after being dragged some distance she was freed, and hiding, made her way to the fort. The son, August, escaped with the Krieger boys to the fort, the daughter Henrietta was captured, and was at Camp Release.

Thiele, (or Tille). There is a lack of detail in regard to this family, and they are not mentioned on the church records. Justina Krieger calls them Tille says they lived "near the woods", that her children found food "at Tille's house", and says that "two of their children, one two, and the other less than a year old, were left at the Krieger home" which was looted and burned shortly after. With this definite data she must have known them intimately. That the father, mother and two children were killed is a fair presumption.

One Wagner, an epileptic brother of Mrs. Kitzman, was killed, and one Untermach is named on the church record as killed.

AT HAWK CREEK.

On the 19th J. H. Ingalls home was attacked and he was killed. Two daughters escaped and joined the J. R. Brown family, in their flight. One daughter Lavinia, and a young son George Washington, were captured. The latter was rescued the next spring, at St. Joseph, by Reverend Fathers Germain and Andre, together with two other young boys: Jimmie Scott captured near Breckenridge, and John Schurch captured at Big Stone Lake. A pony was paid for each boy. Lavinia was rescued near the Missouri river. Mrs. Ingalls was in Wisconsin visiting when the outbreak occurred.

Maj. Joseph R. Brown was the former Indian Agent, married to a daughter of Akipa (Coming together). He was away from home. The family was awakened at about 4 o,clock Tuesday morning by Peter Rouilliard, crying "For God's sake hurry; the Indians are killing everybody". They yoked up three pair of oxen to farm wagons and prepared to leave. There were 26 in the party, they had probably reached the Schwandt place when they were surrounded by Indians led by Shakpi, Marpiya-te-najin, (Stands on a cloud, but commonly called Cut nose), and Dowani-ye (The Singer), three of the worst Indians of the tribes. The pleadings, and threats of vengeance by her Indian relatives, made by Mrs. Brown, and the assistance of an Indian whom she had befriended previously, finally induced the hostiles to order Chas. Holmes, Leopold Wohler, Garvie's cook (at the Upper Agency) and another man, to go and take their chances; which they did and escaped to safety. A German hired man was kept to drive the oxen, Rouilliard was ordered to go back to his Indian wife, while Charles Blair a son-in-law was to be dealt with later. Later, he was disguised as an Indian, taken to the river at night, and told to go. Being in poor health and surrounded by Indians he made poor progress, but finally reached the fort. He never recovered from the exhaustion, but died the following February at Henderson. All others of the Brown family, Mrs. Wohler, and Jennie and Amanda Ingalls were taken prisoners and were at Camp Release. The German teamster, mentioned, escaped from camp during excitement when a white boy was being stoned to death. This boy must have been one whom J. B. Reynolds living at Redwood river, left to bring his team to New Ulm. He has never been accounted for. This ends the murders on August 18th and 19th above the Agency, and on the north side of the river.

MURDERS OPPOSITE THE LOWER AGENCY.

The LaCroix Creek or Birch Coulie settlement was attacked on the morning of the 18th. Mrs. Carl Witt was stacking hay, when shot to death. William a son, was pitching from the load, and jumping off ran to his father. After the Indians left, they returned and buried the body, then fled to the fort.

Eusebius Piquar, was killed, and a daughter Elizabeth was captured, and was at Camp Release. Mrs. Piquar and one child escaped to the fort.

Chas. Clausen, wife and son John, son Frederick with his wife and two children, and a boy Thomas Brook, were starting from their home near Birch Coulie when attacked. Charles and Frederick Clausen and Thomas Brook were killed, Mrs. Frederick and children captured, and the mother and John escaped to the fort.

Ole Samson, wife and two children, were living in their wagon. Ole was cutting hay when killed. The savages set fire to the wagon with the mother and children in it. Their attention being diverted, Mrs. Samson jumped from the wagon with a child in her arms, and hiding in the brush made her way to Fort Ridgely.

Thomas Smith and family were moving to their claim at the mouth of LaCroix Creek. Having left his son John, with the cattle at Christian Schlumbergers' on the way, he started with his son William, in the morning of the 18th, to go back for them, but reaching a point just below Magners, they were informed of the outbreak. The father started back for the family, and mistaking Indians at the Magner house, went up to them and was killed with tomahawks. Wllliam stopped to talk with Magner's son, before following his father, when the boys saw three Indians in warpaint coming up a ravine. They ran toward the fort, and reaching Schlumbergers' escaped with them to Fort Ridgely. Mrs. Smith and daughter Mary 5 years old, were warned and fled through the brush to the fort.

Edward Magner, Patrick Kelly and David Mc Connell, sent their families to the fort, staying behind to care for the stock. All three were killed.

Peter Pereau was killed at his home, but the family escaped to the fort.

John Buehro was killed; his wife and infant got to the fort.

Henry Kaertner; was killed the wife escaped to Fort Ridgely.

William Taylor, a colored man from St. Paul, was killed while fleeing from the Agency.

MASSACRES ABOUT NEW ULM.

At Milford, just west of New Ulm, were more people killed than in any other township, the number being 51, and of these 21 were related. Two others from Leavenworth were killed here. After the murders at the Agency, bands immediately left for the settlements. The murders at Milford will never be adequately described, as but few escaped, and few, if any made prisoners. Most of the information came from a mulatto named Godfrey, at the Indian trials. This miserable creature has been held up as a devil incarnate in the histories, but as a matter of fact was a "scared stiff nigger", and well he might be, with the company he was in. Nine of the 38 Indians hung at Mankato, were in his party. It was on his testimony that most of them were hung; he was a scared Negro and told all he knew. His sentence was 10 years imprisonment, but he was pardoned and sent to Crow Creek with the others in 1866. The list of families is as follows:.

Wilson Massipost, and two daughters Mary and Julia were the first victims of this party. Massipost was a widower. A young boy escaped.

Anton Messmer, wife Mary Anne, were killed in the field. A son Joseph, was wounded in escaping, and was left on the roadside for dead; he was picked up but died the next day.

Adolph Schilling, and a daughter Louise; were killed, but the wife and son Joseph ran into the cornfield and escaped.

Anton Henle kept a stopping place called "The Travelers' Home" on the river road, and on this morning was returning from New Ulm, accompanied by several teams carrying a party of men recruiting volunteers for southern service. Henle was driving ahead, and near his home, saw his brother-in-law Joseph Messmer lying by the road. He stopped and two other teams passed him. They saw the Indians and thinking to scare them, yelled and drove toward them. More Indians sprang up from hiding places and opened fire. Julius Fenske tried to turn his team about, but was shot and killed. All then jumped out and ran back, while the Indians caught the teams. A. Diederich and John Schneider were killed and Adolph Steinle so badly wounded that he died in a few days, The rest of the party fled to New Ulm with the terrible news. Mrs. Henle had gone to her mother's, Mrs. Messmer, and as she approached her the mother was shot down. She turned and ran to her home where she found three Indians who tried to sieze her, but she eluded them and hid in the brush until evening when the husband found her. Anton aged 8, and Mary 4 years, were killed. Martin, 12

years old was badly wounded and died two weeks
later, leaving the family childless.

At Joseph Stocker's, the wife Caroline nee Zich-
er was sick in bed, when Wapa-duta (Scarlet leaf),
the father-in-law of Godfrey shot through a window
killing her. Stocker and a neighbor girl Cecelia Ochs
ran into the cellar stairway, and the Indians fearing
that he had a gun, did not enter, but set the house
afire and went on. Stocker and the girl dug their
way out under the foundation and escaped.

Florian Hartman, and his helper John Rohner,
were shot down in the field. Hartman's wife Maria
nee Henle, hearing shooting went to the field to see
what the disturbance was. She found Rohner dead,
and Hartman a short distance away mortally wounded. He begged of her to hide in the corn. She
was unable to drag him away, and while they talked
Indians came and fired into Rohner's body. Seeing
that she could not aid him, and knowing that her
presence was likely to attract attention, she hid in
the corn. Returning later she found him dead. In
the neighborhood she remained, though she went to
New Ulm and finding it deserted, came back, until
on the 17th day she was discovered by her brother
Athanasius Henle. She supposed the country was
deserted, and was storing supplies for winter.

Sebastian Mey, wife Barbara, son Henry, and an
infant were killed. A young daughter, Anne Mary,
and Magadalena and Charles, twins of about three
years were left for dead, but were revived next day,

by a rescue party and taken to New Ulm. Just at the time of the attack Carl Heuyers and Joseph Emery of Leavenworth, drove into Mey's yard, and were killed and the team taken.

Benedict Drexler was killed in his field, and his head was cut off and carried away, The wife Margaretha, and Mary 9, Ursula 7, Matilda 6, and Cresentia 4 years old hid in the cornfield and escaped.

Of the others killed in Milford, but little can be told, but the list is as follows:

John Zettel. wife Barbara, children Lizzette 8, Stephen 5, Anton 4, and a babe 2, years old were killed; extinguishing the family.

Max Zeller, wife Lucretia, Pauline, Theresa, Max and an infant; entire family.

John Martin Fink, wife Monica and son Max.

John Schwartz, wife Anna Maria, and daughter Katherine, evidently fled as far as the Apfelbaum farm in Courtlandt, where they were killed.

John Gluth, Mr. Belzer, Max Haag, Jacob Keck, Martin Merkle, Joseph Pelzl and wife Margaret and Mr. Thilling and wife.

MURDERS OPPOSITE FORT RIDGELY.

J. B. Reynolds kept a stopping place near the mouth of the Redwood River, and stopping with his family were LeGrand Davies, Mary E. Schwandt who lived at Middle Creek, Mattie Williams, Mary Anderson and a boy, not named. Reynolds took his wife in his buggy and escaped by the aid of Indians, to the fort. The boy was left to drive a team down;

it is probable that he was killed at Little Crow's village on Wednesday morning. Francois Patoille, a trader, took the others in his wagon, while Antoine LeBlanc rode on horseback. They were warned by Indians, and drove around the Agency on the prairie; when at a point opposite the fort, on the New Ulm road, they were attacked by the Indians who committed the Milford murders, and the men were killed. Mary Anderson was badly wounded, and died in a few days. The other two were at Camp Release

IN LEAVENWORTH TOWNSHIP.

The murders in this region were comitted from Monday 18th to Sunday 25th, and scarcely a witness escaped. The district lies southwest of New Ulm.

John Bluem, wife and five children, were driving to New Ulm for safety. The parents, and Margaret, Elizabeth, Charles and Adam, were killed. A son John, Jr., escaped.

Seth Henshaw was driving to New Ulm, with a Mrs. Harrington and two children, and a Mrs. Hill. Henshaw was killed, and Mrs. Harrington and the younger child slightly wounded. They were all thrown from the wagon, and escaped in the brush, while the Indians caught the team. Mrs. Hill with one child got to New Ulm; the mother and wounded child wandered for eight days, finally reaching Col. Flandreau's camp, midway of New Ulm and Mankato, at Crisp's farm.

The home of Heydrick was attacked, and the

wife and two children were killed. Heydrick narrowly escaped by jumping from a bridge and hiding in a ravine.

Carl Heuyer, (killed at Milford), was absent when his wife Hannah and sons Carl and John were killed at the home.

Philetus Jackson, his wife and son were fleeing to New Ulm, when Jackson was killed.   The others hid in the brush and escaped.

Joseph Emery was killed at Milford.

Ruth VanGuilder-Howard, an aged woman was wounded while escaping, and died next morning.

George Roesser and wife were killed at their home, and an 18 months old babe was left for dead, but was rescued on Tuesday.

Elijah Whiton, wife, daughter and son, lived near Heydrick, and paid no attention to rumors, but saw Indians chasing Heydrick on Thursday.   Whiton hid the family and went to warn his brother Luther.   Not returning, they fled to New Ulm.   Later, Whiton returned and searched in vain for the family. He then started for New Ulm.   Falling in with Wm. J. Duly, who escaped at Lake Shetek, they were in the deserted home of Henry Thomas, when Indians came and killed Whiton; Duly escaped.

Joseph Brown, kept a stopping place on the road to Lake Shetek. He was a widower, and had a grown daughter Oratia, and son Jonathan F.   They were all found dead.

In Nicollet county near New Ulm, several were

killed, but most escaped. Dickinson on his way to
St. Peter from the fort gave warning.

Jacob Mauerle had taken his family to St. Peter
but returned on Friday and was killed and horribly
mutilated.

John and Christopher Apfelbaum, fled from the
farm home, but were killed near St. Peter. Their
bodies were found the following spring. It was at
or near this farm that the John Schwarz family were
killed while fleeing from Milford.

Charles Nelson lived at Norwegian Grove, and
fled with his children to the cornfield, as the Indians
killed his wife. Returning a few days later he discovered that his two young sons, from whom he had
become separated in flight were alive and uninjured.
The ills of this family led to the writing of the song
"What cares Laughing Minnehaha for the corpses in
the Vail," once so popular.

One Gilligan, and three unnamed Germans, left
the Riggs party who fled from the Upper Agency, and
were killed in this neighborhood the 23d. Others,
of whom details are lacking, are August Nierenz,
Frederick G. Gerboth and Wm. Sonnenburg.

COTTONWOOD RESCUE PARTY.

Settlers on the Cottonwood river, came into
New Ulm to verify reports of Indian trouble, and
learning the real state of affairs, a party of 16 men
went out on Tuesday to warn and rescue the people.
Part were on horseback the rest in wagons. They
discovered many of the murdered, and at the home

of Sebastian Mey revived three of his children who had been left for dead. At the home of Geo. Roesser they found an 18 months old child, the only survivor, trying to get water from a pail. These were sent to New Ulm. A Thomas Ryan (or Riant), who had previously escaped an attack by Indinas, was discovered hiding in the brush, and joined the party. When returning to New Ulm they divided into two parties, one on each side of the river, agreeing to meet and enter town together. The party with the wagons did not wait, but proceeded to town. While crossing a marsh, near the present hospital, they were attacked and several killed. The other party coming along later saw Indians, but determined to fight their way through. As they reached the same spot all but one were killed. Almond and Uriah Loomis, DeWitt Lemon, Thomas Ryan, Nels, Tork and Ole Olson, Jan Tomson, Wm. Tuttle, George Lamb and Wm. B. Carroll were killed. Those who escaped were: Robert Kirby, Samuel McAuliffe, Luther C. Ives, Ralph Thomas, Robert Henton and —— Kuhn. This same evening a young girl, Emilie Pauley was shot down on the street opposite the Dakota house. No further attack was made.

BATTLE AT NEW ULM.

On Saturday August 23d, scouts reported the Indians approaching in large numbers; preparations were made to meet them. Some eight blocks of the town had been barricaded, and 175 well armed men had come in from surrounding towns; though some

75 had gone to the LaFayette district, and were unable to return.   About 200 buildings were burned to prevent shelter for the savages.   The Indians did not attempt to rush the town, but lying concealed, kept up a firing during the day and night, withdrawing on Sunday morning.   The killed numbered 26, of whom eight were residents.   Two Indians were killed.   The list is given in the appendix.

There are several accounts written in a very graphic style, and undoubtedly it was a terrible occasion.   The town was overcrowded with refugees and volunteer defenders.   Many were wounded, sick or exhausted from recent flights to safety.   Scarcely a person not in mourning.   The defense was another example of unpreparedness.   Many had pitchforks and butcher-knives for weapons.   Most were armed with shotguns or hunting rifles.   The Indians with the muskets captured at the ferry battle, did deadly work beyond rifle range   Many were desperate to foolhardiness, and there was no real management or co-operation.   Two Indians were killed: Cink-pa, (Tree tops), and Wasicun, (Le Blanc or Provencalle) all meaning "White man", a French breed.

Upper Agency and Settlements.

So soon as the massacre was commenced at the Agency, messengers started to the Yellow Medicine or Upper Agency, spreading the news by the way. George Gleason, clerk for Agent Galbraith, was returning to the Lower Agency, accompanied by the wife and children of Dr. Wakefield the Upper Agency physician, and when near Redwood river, two Indians met them and killed Gleason and took the others prisoners. They were at Camp Release. Except as Chaska and Hepan, (1st and 2d sons, these are not identified. Both were hung at Mankato.

Rev. Amos Huggins, at Lac qui Parle, brought his oxen in, and while unhooking them was shot and killed. With this murderer, was Tate-kage "Wind Maker" a son of a friendly headman Wakan-Tanka, "Great Spirit"; despite his being only 14 years old, and partially demented he was hung at Mankato. Wakan-Tanka cared for Mrs. Huggins and children until they were rescued by Sibley.

Pahatka, "Stroking against the grain", was the messenger to the Upper Agency, and after being joined by several lower Indians, at evening they looted and burned the stores. James W. Lindsay,

Louis Constans, and Chas. Lauer were killed, and Stewart B. Garvie wounded so that he died. The Agency employes and others to the number of 62 people were guided to Hutchinson, by John Other Day, a Sisseton married to a white woman. This man Anpetu-to-kecha, was a remarkable Indian. He was a fighter, and in a quarrel with Marpiya-te-nazin (Stands on a cloud), bit off a part of his antagonist's nose. This was the bloody Cut Nose who "killed white people till his arm was tired" in the massacre; he was tried and hung.

Dr. Williamson and Rev. S. R. Riggs, missionaries, with all their families and friends were secretly aided to escape by friendly Indians, members of the Mission.

New stores were building at Big Stone Lake, on which a number of men were employed, and the following were killed, on Aug. 21-22: Alexis Dubuque, Geo. Loth, Frank Peshette, —— Laundre, —— Ryder, —— Patnode; in a haying camp near, Hillias and Henry Manderffeld. A boy, John Schurch, was taken prisoner. Five men escaping from this locality joined the Riggs missionary party; four of these were killed near New Ulm; a wounded man named Orr remained with the Riggs' to St. Peter. Anton Manderfield escaped at the haying camp. Thus only two escaped, though Schurch was bought from Indians as before related. Peter Guilbault was a victim, but particulars are unknown. There were no settlements above the Agency, and the victims were living in work camps for Daileys & Pratt building a trading post at Big Stone Lake, which accounts for meagre information. A band led by Wan-hde-ga, (Striped arrow), a member of Inkpa-duta's band, were the murderers in this region.

MASSACRE AT LAKE SHETEK.

At this lake in Murray county, some 70 miles southwest of New Ulm, the following settlers with their families, had located: John Eastlick, Phineas B. Hurd, John Wright, Wm. J. Duly, H. W. Smlth, Wm. Everett, Thomas Ireland, Andrew Koch; and also, Charles Hatch, William Jones. Edgar Bentley, John Vought, E. G. Koch, John F., and Daniel Burns all single men. Hurd and Jones left for a months trip to the Missouri river, on June 2d, but were never heard from. The Indians came to the Hurd home and shot and killed Vought, who was working there, as he stepped out of the door with an infant in his arms. Mrs. Hurd coming out, was ordered to take her children and "go to her mother"; she was not allowed to take a wrap or food. She made her way under many difficulties to New Ulm, after many days. She claims to have recognized her husband's horse and dog among those of the Indians. This was in the early morning. The next place visited was Koch's, where they killed him and took the wife prisoner. Charles Hatch coming to Hurds saw them shoot Koch, and ran back to spread the alarm. The settlers gathered at the home of Wright. Several Indians were camped near this

place, who first appeared friendly, but later joined in
the killing; the headman was known as "Pawn" to
the settlers.   It is almost certain that he was Inkpa-
duta (Scarlet point), the leader of the Spirit Lake
massacre in 1857; the others were led by Wake
ska (White Lodge), another band living separate
from the tribes.

At first it was intended to defend the house, but
on the Indians threatening to burn it, the party left
it and started toward New Ulm.   The Indians followed, and finally began shooting at them.   H. W.
Smith and a man named Forbes deserted the party,
though both well armed.   The balance fled to the
high grass of a marsh, and put up a feeble defense,
against superior numbers.   Old "Pawn" now assum-
ed the leadership, and called to the women and children to come out and they would not be harmed.
Eastlick had been killed, Everett and Ireland severely
wounded, leaving only Duly, Hatch and Bentley
for defense.   Knowing they would be taken, dead or
alive, and hoping that some might be spared, the
women and children went out to the Indians, except
a few children.   Immediately after starting off with
the prisoners the carnage began; they were shot to
death, till only seven remained; Mrs. Eastlick being
brutally beaten and left for dead.

When the Indians left, after firing many shots
at the men concealed in the marsh, W. J. Duly, the
only man unwounded, deserted his companions and
started for New Ulm.   There is somthing peculiar

about this man's adventures.   Mato-ma-hucha, (Lean Bear), was killed by a settler whom he tried to warn of danger. and it is claimed that Duly killed him.   He is said to have joined Elijah Whiton on the way to New Ulm; they were attacked and Whiton was killed.   He was selected to cut the rope on the drop which hung the Indians at Mankato, and was so frightened he succeeded only by accident. An officer describes him as the "blackest white man he ever saw", and says he missed the rope at the signal and accidentally touched the taut rope in his exment, severing it.

Everett badly wounded, assisted by Hatch and Bentley, both slightly wounded, made their way to a road-house known as "Dutch Charley's" and later were joined by Ireland, seriously wounded, and Merton Eastlick and his baby brother Johnnie, whom he had carried on his back all the way.   A hard feat for a 14-year old boy.   Later they were joined by Mrs. Eastlick who had been left for dead. Mrs. Hurd and two children, and Aaron Meyers and wife were in this party, which was rescued by soldiers under Capt. Dane and taken to Mankato.

Mrs. Wright and one child. Mrs. Duly and two children, Lillian Everett and two young daughters of Ireland were carried to the village of White Lodge on the Missouri river.   How Mrs. Cook and a son of Wright were separated from them and were at Camp Release, is not explained.

Four Bears, Martin Charger, Kills and comes,

Swift Bird, Mad Bear, Pretty Bear, Sitting Bear, One Rib, Strikes Fire, Red Dog and Charging Dog, friendly Dakotas, undertook the recovery of these captives. They were joined by On-spe-ni, (Don't know how), Chased by a Ree Indian and Fast walker, members of another band. On-spe-ni, who is known as D. K. How, tells the following interesting story; "We started from our camp at Swan lake, near Standing Rock, with these people, (Indians) who came there on their way to buy the captives with ponies. We got to White Lodge's camp, and we put our horses right in front—the horses we were going to buy the captives with—and White Lodge's people gave us a feast, and we had a meeting, but White Lodge was not there. After a while each one brought a captive and took a horse away, but still White Lodge did not appear. Chased by a Ree got up and spoke this wise: "Where are you White Lodge? These are men, good men; come to us as men. Why don't you come out and do as a man?" Soon a white woman came out and came to the meeting, and her tears ran down her face. She was not my relative but I felt very bad, and my heart was coming up to my throat. This man Fast walker had his gun ready and I had my knife in my belt. We did not know but we might have some trouble, and so we were prepared. As soon as we got all the captives we came away. This white woman, that came in crying, was White Lodge's wife; he would not let her go. We took away eight captives, and went back to

Green Plank creek and camped. Next morning, just as we were ready to start, White Lodge appeared. We made ready to kill him, if necessary; but he did not walk fast, and we walked faster than he did, finally he went back. We came on to Swan Lake, where we started from; the other Indians then took the captives along."

The captives, Mrs. Wright and daughter, Mrs. Duly and two children, two daughters of Ireland and Lillie Everett, were delivered to Major Galpin, at Fort Pierre, and returned to their relatives. The following is a list by families:

John Eastlick, sons Fred, Giles and Frank were killed; Mrs. Eastlick, Merton and Johnnie escaped.

W. J. Duly escaped, wife and two children prisoners; children Willie and Belle killed.

Phineas Hurd, undoubtedly killed; Mrs. Hurd and two children escaped.

John Wright away from home; Mrs. Wright and two children prisoners. One child at Camp Release.

H. W. Smith escaped, the wife was killed near the slough.

Wm. Everett escaped, Lillie taken prisoner; the wife, son Charles and an infant son killed after surrender of women and children.

Thomas Ireland escaped; wife killed after surrender; two girls, prisoners; two children killed.

Andrew Koch killed; wife was prisoner at Camp Release.

John Vought, killed; William Jones killed with with Hurd; Bentley and Hatch escaped.

MURDERS IN KANDIYOHI COUNTY.

On Wednesday August 20th, a number of Scandinavian settlers were gathered at the home of Andreas Lundborg, near Norway Lake, for religious services. Children came from the homes, reporting that Indians were committing depredations there, The people started for their homes. Andreas Lundborg and four sons, at whose home the meeting was held, accompanied the Andreas and Daniel Broberg families. They were attacked on the way and the following were killed:

Sons of Andreas Lundborg—Anders Peter, Gustav and Lars.

Andreas Broberg, wife Christina, sons Johannes and Andreas, daughter Christina; only Anna Stina, aged 16 years escaped.

Daniel Broberg, wife Anna Stina, sons Alfred and John Albert; Anders Peter escaped. A third brother, Johannes, recently arrived from Norway, was also killed. The women and children were beaten to death with guns or hatchets; the body of Daniel was nearly burned up,

Four Indians came to the home of Lars Endreson near Eagle Lake on the 21st, and after shaking hands, shot him to death, and wounded a young son Ole. Two young daughters Guri and Brita, they were made prisoner, while the mother Gudre, with baby

Anna, hid in the cellar. Endre, the oldest son, returning from an errand, was killed in the door-yard. The Indians then left, taking the girls along. Later on the girls escaped to Forest City. Gudre hid in the brush that night and going to the house found Ole, who had revived, trying to get a meal. She hitched the oxen to a sled, the only conveyance, and started for Oscar Erickson's, a son-in-law, five miles away. Here were Solomon Foote and Erickson both badly wounded. Foote and wife, and Carl Carlson went there on the 20th, after hearing reports of an outbreak. Indians came and camped near that night apparently friendly, but next morning killed Carlson, and wounded Foote and Erickson. Foote was again wounded, but with his wife's assistance, drove them off. As the women could not move the wounded men, it was decided that they should go to Forest City for help, which they did.

When Mrs, Endreson approached the place, she heard strange noises; fearing Indians, she hid in the brush over night. Next morning, the 23d, Ole was seen by Erickson, who called to him. Gudre then hitched to a wagon, and drove the party to Forest City where they found the others.

A party of fleeing settlers were attacked near the present site of Atwater, on the 21st. They were bringing their cattle along, and in an attempt to save them, Sven Helgeson Backlund and Andreas Lorentson, two aged men, were killed and their bodies horridly mutilated.

Others killed, of which no particulars are found, were: Carl Peter Jonason the father of Carl Carlson, Johannes Iverson, Berger Tollerson, Olof Olson Haugan, wife Bergeret and son Frederick.   The most of the settlers fled to Forest City, some to Paynesville, and a few secreted themselves on an island in Norway Lake and were rescued later.   Although many of these settlers were shooting at Indians, there is no evidence that any were killed except "one was killed in the Big Woods", of which name, place and date are lacking.   A log fort was built at Forest City, the logs set on end and over-lapping.   The place was attacked, some stock driven off, several wounded, but no fatalities.

Forest City was the largest settlement in Meeker County, and the number gathered there, made it necessary to bring in food.   A foraging party was attacked at Mannanah township and Phillip Deck, Linus Howe, Wilmot Maybee and Joseph Page were killed, on August 27th.   Nels Olson, blacksmith, and Daniel Cross of Hutchinson, were killed at Lake Ripley, date uncertain.

At Hutchinson, McLeod County, John Adams and family going to town were attacked on August 20th; a child was brained over a wagon wheel, and the wife Minnie taken prisoner.   John escaped.   On Sept. 4th, August Spaude and family approached town while the Indians were attacking it.   Spaude was killed and his body fell in the river.   The wife with two children escaped while Indians caught the team. She endeavored to enter the town, but was killed with children near the Asa Hutchinson place. At Lake Addie, probably Sept. 23d, Samuel White, wife, son Otis and daughter Susan were murdered. Caleb Sanborn and A. S. Cant were killed while out scouting during September.

JACKSON COUNTY MASSACRE.

It is strange that mention of these people is not made in any massacre history. There is no doubt of the facts; the matter is fully detailed in Rose' History of Jackson County, and a monument has been erected bearing the names of the victims.

In the present Belmont township a colony of Norwegians from Iowa had settled. On August 25th they were attacked, and the following were killed: Johannes Axe, Mikkel Olson Slaabaken, Ole Fohre, Lars Furnes, Knud Langeland, Nicolai John Langeland, wife Anna, daughters Anna and Agaata, Lars G. Jornevik and wife, Knut and Brita Midstad. After beating the Indians off, the survivors fled back to Iowa. In all likehood this was the work of Inkpaduta's band. Perhaps a description of this band is of interest. Wamdi-sapa (Black Eagle), with about 12 lodges broke away from the Wapa-kutas in early days, and was killed or died in 1848, when his son Inkpa-duta became chief. The band in 1849 murdered a Wapaton chief Wa-wamdi-a-akapi and 17 warriors, near Bear Lake, Murray County. In 1857 they committed the Spirit Lake massacre. They undoubtedly participated at Lake Shetek. They were camped near the band of Tatanka-najin (Standing Buffalo), a peaceful Sisseton, with whom Sibley was about to hold a council in July 1863, at Big Mound, Dakota. Sibley scouts were shaking hands with members of Standing Buffalo's band, when a member of this renegade band shot and killed Dr. J. S. Weiser, a surgeon on Sibley's staff, and precipitated the battle. The band was in the Custer massacre. Following this they fled to Canada, where Inkpa-duta died in 1879.

VARIOUS MURDERS 1862-3-4-5.

Blue Earth County, vicinity of Cambria, on Sept. 9, 1862: John Armstrong, Thomas J. Davis, James Edwards, John S. Jones, Jonas Mohr,.

August 11, 1864, same locality, Chas. C. Mack and Noble G. Root.

On May 2d, 1865, a band of marauder murdered Andrew J. Jewett, his wife, his father and mother, and a hired man, Charles Tyler, at the Jewett home and a boy Frank York in the neighborhood. John Campbell, a son of Scott Campbell for a long time interpreter at Fort Snelling, and a brother to Baptiste who was hung at Mankato, was one of this party. He was captured, given a brief trial in an impromptu court, and hanged from a handy tree.

Henry Bosche was killed on the Pfaender farm near New Ulm in May 1863.

Watonwan County victims of whom there is no data, were —— Patterson and child, Gabriel Ellingson, —— Peterson, Ole and Gilbert Palmer, and and Christian Roland, during 1862-3.

Near Smith Lake, in Wright County, on June 29, 1863, a small band of marauders attacked a family named Dustin. They were moving westward and were shot with bullet or arrow, or beaten to death. Amos, his mother Jeanette, and his son Robert were killed outright. The ox team ran back and went to the home of M. V. Cochrane where they were recognized and a hunt was started. Kate with her two children Almeda 6, and Leon 2 years old, were found just west of present Howard Lake. She was shot through with a steel-pointed arrow, but had traveled some three miles before giving out. She died from wounds and exhaustion July 3d.

James A. McGannon; coming from Forest City, was shot from his horse and killed by Indians near Lake Sylvia, on July 1, 1863. It was probably the Dustin murderers who killed him. They were members of Little Crow's band, who had come back for the purpose of stealing horses. Heyoka (Clown), a son-in-law of Crow was with the party and took Mc Gannon's coat which Crow was wearing when killed.

A number were killed in the vicinity of Fort Abercrombie on the river near Breckenridge, but the details are very sparse. Following is the list, most of whom were killed during September 1862, but died later from wounds:

Austin, Andrew   Mayo, H. H.,   Siegel, William
Bennett, James   Russell, Edw'd   Snell, Chas. W.

Battins, Chas.   Ryan (or Scott) Steele, Edw'd D.
Evans, (mail c'r) Schulz, William   Wright, Edwd M.
Fehrenbach, M. Wensinger John, Ruchenell, Aug'sts
    The following are scattered victims: J. B. Van
Eaton, near Grove Lake, Stearns Co., May 1863.
Silas Foote, brother of Solomon, near Lightning lake
in Ottertail Co., May 3, J863.

It has been claimed that there were many people not named, killed at various times and locations
but a search of several years, assisted by many participants has failed to reveal them   The following
corrections and additions to history we wish to note:
Massacre of 13 persons at Belmont, Jackson Co.—
Benj Juni, Sr., and John Schmerch (Schurch) were
not killed—Lathrop Dickson, at Lower Agency, and
an unnamed boy at Little Crow's camp were victims,
another was Eliphalet Richardson near Ft. Ridgely.
—we take credit for the only account of victims at
Sacred Heart and Middle Creek.   To the following
informants we acknowledge cur deep obligations for
kind and gratuitous assistance: William Wiehman,
Frank Shoemaker, Joseph Crusoll, R. D. Hinman,
Louis Kitzman, Mrs. Owen Carrigan (Carrothers),
and Mrs. Michael Belter.   Congressman George R.
Smith for public documents, to Dr. Wm. W. Folwell
for assistance in many ways, and to Samuel J. Brown
and Thomas A. Robertson for favors beyond our
ability to repay.

The Battles at Fort Ridgely.

There has been much absurd matter published describing the skulking Indians in battle as an army, and the chiefs and headmen as commanders. This gives an entirely wrong impression. Indians do not fight en masse, but rather each singly. No orders are given, more than in a mob. While there may be agreement as to some things, it may or may not be carried out. While Little Crow may have exhorted he could not command and enforce obedience, as is frequently shown. Only two Indians were killed at each battle, Ridgely, New Ulm and Birch Coulie. This was owing to the fact that they kept out of range, unless fully concealed and protected. Such a thing as an advance in face of danger is not found in Indian tactics. Skulking and sneaking to places of advantage, each fought his own battle.

Fort Ridgely was more fit for a county fair than for a fort. It stood on high ground about one mile from the river, a square of wooden buildings, except one, open on the river side. The cannon were under charge of novices, lately trained, but served to keep the Indians at a safe distance, and prevented a general attack. They laid under cover and kept up an irregular firing at long range. Any history will give a very graphic account of the battle, so details are omitted here. Robert Baker, Co. I, 10th Regt., carelessly exposed himself at a window and was shot down. Wm. Goodie Co. C., and Mark M. Greer, Co. B, 5th Regt., were killed in action. Heinrich Reike, died from heart failure induced by fright, and Felix Smith and Onesime Vanasse were killed in trying to enter the fort. Two Indians were killed: Ho-hpi-maza, (Iron Nest) and Upi-hde-ga (Striped wing feather), both members of Shak-pi's band.

It was no easy thing to control matters during the several days of fighting and watchfulness at the fort. Much credit is due Timothy J. Sheehan who was in command. Most of his troop were new recruits, the citizens were panic-stricken farmers and laborers, unfit for service. Huddled in the barracks were about 180 soldiers and over 200 fugitives, who were bereaved, wounded, physically exhausted or otherwise incapacitated. Had the Indians pushed the attack, there would have been as much to fear from panic as from the foe. The "big guns" scared the Indians so that they kept back. The muskets secured from the ferry battle, were their only guns to be feared. It was a fortunate ending to a terrible event, much to the credit of the defenders.

THE BIRCH COULIE BATTLE.

On August 31st, the fort garrison having been sufficiently re-inforced, Col. Sibley sent out a burial and relief party under Maj. Jos. R. Brown, to cover the Agency territory. Capt. Hiram P. Grant was in command of the troop, consisting of Co. A, 6th Regt. and some 70 mounted men under Capt. Joseph Anderson, and a number of citizens. The party went up the river on the north side, and after burying a number of bodies, encamped opposite the Redwood Agency. Next morning the party divided, and the mounted men crossed at the Agency, going up the south side of the river, while the rest covered the north side taking in the settlements at LaCroix Creek, Birch Coulie, and about Beaver Falls; the parties united and went into camp about two miles north of present Morton. From all reports, and as a matter of fact, the Indians had gone up to Yellow Medicine, and the camp was poorly chosen, and improperly guarded. A war party coming down the river discovered mounted men and sent scouts to mark their movements, who reported where they had camped. It was decided to attack the camp at daybreak. Little Crow, disgusted and disheartened at the opposition among the Indians, and by the active preparation by the whites, had taken his chosen followers and gone north to forage and steal horses. The attack was led by Gray Bird, Hu-shasha (Red Legs), Wamdi-tanka (Big Eagle), and Maka-to (Blue Eath). The coulie on the north, prairie swells on the south and west gave the Indians natural barricades, from which they poured in a terrible cross-fire on the whites, as the alarm was given in the morning by the firing of pickets. As the men sprang to their feet, many were shot down, and the horses all soon killed; some 90 horses. The soldiers then dug pits, and vigorously fought off their assailants, so there were small casualties after the first assault. All day long there was desultory fighting. The reports of volley firing reached the fort, and Sibley dispatched Col. McPhail with 240 men and two howitzer to the relief of the command. Late in the afternoon McPhail came up within about a mile of the battle ground, and when Maka-to with less than 100 warriors disputed his passage, fired a few shots and retired about two miles, sending back for re-inforcements. Most histories sarcastically allude to this performance, and it was peculiar. A command but slightly over half his force had battled the Indians all day, holding their ground, of which he was now in sight. His casualties were two horses killed—no one wounded—yet he left the beleagured band to fight it out alone. Next morning Sibley with his entire command came and the Indians fled. The losses were, Co. A 6th Regt.: Sergt. John College, Corp. Wm. Cobb, Geo. Colter, Chauncey L. King, Wm. Russell, Henry Whetsler; Co. G. 6th Regt.: Sergt. Benj. S. Terry, Corp. F. C. W. Bennekin; Cullen Guards: Sergt. Robt. Baxter, Peter Bourrier, Richard Gibbons and Jacob Freeman. Died later C. F. Coyle, Wm. Irvine; Henry Rolleau Co. A 6th and Joseph Kellene Co. A 9th Regt. Citizens killed: J. C. Dickinson, J. W. DeCamp and S. R. Hender-

son. Indians killed: Wan-i-he-ya (Shoots the arrow), and Ho-ton-na (Animals' voice).

After the battle Sibley, hoping to open communication with Little Crow, left the following note, so
that it was found by the Indians.

"If Little Crow has any proposition to make, let
him send a half-breed to me, and he shall be protected
in and out of camp "

Just previous to this note, Little Crow had proposed making peace, to the band which accompanied
him to the big woods, but they would not consent to
it. Their view was clearly stated by Marpiya-na-
xtan-xtan at their council:

"It cannot be done! We have gone too far! Since
the treaties (1851), when did we do the least thing, either stealing cattle or in harming a white man, that we
did not get punished for? Now, the Indians have been
killing men, women and children, how many—God only
knows—and if we give ourselves up we shall all be
hung."

It was several days before an answer was sent to
Sibley, carried by Thos. A. Robertson and Thomas
Robinson, mixed-bloods, as follows:

"For what reason we have commenced this war I
will tell you. It is on account of Maj. Galbraith. We
made a treaty with the government, and beg for what
little we do get, and can't get it till our children are dying with hunger. It was with the Traders that it commenced. Mr. A. J. Myrick told the Indians 'they could
eat grass or their own dung'. Then Mr. Forbes told
the Lower Indians 'they were not men'. Then Robert
was making with his friends how to defraud us of our
money. If the young men have pushed the white men

I have done this myself. So I want you to let Gov.
Ramsey know this. I have a great many prisoners women and children. It ain't all our fault, the Winne-
bagos were in the engagement, two of them was killed.
I want you to give me answer by bearer. All at present. Yours truly, friend Little Crow."

This letter plainly stated the Indian grievances,
and the Indian determination to fight it out, and
none understood it so well as Sibley; the messengers
brought also a clandestine message from Wapa-sha
and Taopi, two Lower chiefs expressing opposition
to the outbreak, and seeking means of escape from
the hostile camp. This must have made evident to
Sibley the discord among the Indians, and probably
had a large bearing on his much maligned policy of
slow and sure moving. No credit is given the friendly Indians for their part in massacre settlement, but
they were at least the second factor in the collapse
of hostilities. Before the battle of Wood Lake they
had threatened to whip Little Crow and take his
prisoners from him.

THE BATTLE AT ACTON.

When news of the outbreak came to the Govern-
or, Capt. Richard Strout of Minneapolis was ordered
to recall the furloughed men of his newly organized
Co. B, 9th Regt., enlist civilians sufficient to form
e company, and to report to Col. J. H. Stevens at
Glencoe. He impressed teams and provisions and
enlisted civilian volunteers, and left Minneapolis on
August 26th. He marched up the west side of the

Mississippi to Clearwater, thence to Forest City, and by way of Hutchinson to Glencoe. On reaching Glencoe, and seeing no signs of Indians, the company was ordered back to Forest City, as depredations were reported from that locality. Return was planned by way of Hutchinson, Cedar Lake and Acton. Leaving Hutchinson on Sept. 2d, they lost some time repairing the road, and finally camped at the Robinson Jones place at Acton. The camp was in the dense woods, guards poorly placed, and only Dakota superstition against fighting in the dark or with a concealed enemy, saved the command from complete destruction. Their presence was known and escaped guarde before midnight.

     Capt. Geo. C. Whitcomb, and his Forest City company returning from scouting near Diamond Lake discovered Indians in force and had an encounter with them some three miles north of the Jones' place, and retreated to their Forest City stockade. He found there a message from Strout, saying that his company would camp that night at Jones' place in Acton. Knowing that Strout was in imminent danger and probably unaware of it, Whitcomb called for volunteer scouts to carry him a warning. Jesse Branham, Jr., Thos. G. Holmes and Albert H. Sperry accepted the mission. Riding to the east, then circling southwest these scouts came to the camp on the road by which the company entered, and hailed a much surprised guard. Strout was awakened and informed of conditions. A council resulted in the decision to avoid the Indians, who greatly outnumbered them, and retire by the way the scouts had entered. Their reserve ammunition was examined, and it was discovered that the musket-balls must be hammered to an oblong shape to fit the old Belgian muskets they carried; and this was done. Camp was broken at daylight and the march was started. When about a mile from the woods, on the open prairie, the scouts discovered Indians in a wheatfield and preparations for fighting were made. An Indian said to have been Little Crow, got up on the fence and waved blanket signals, and shortly a large body of Indians emerged from the woods which the company had just left, and endeavored to attack on each flank and the rear. Forming his company in the hollow-square order the Indians were pushed back and the advance continued for several miles, when the fight became a harrassed retreat into Hutchinson. Edwin Stone, Geo. W. Gideon and Alva Getchell were killed and left on the field; 17 men were wounded, including Scout Branham, and nine teams and the supplies were lost. It is said that an Indian was killed, but the report is not yet verified.

As this was a Minneapolis company and has received very crude notice in history, we print the roster of the company. The list has never been accurately filed at the State office; the roster here given was taken from various sources, and approved at a meeting of survivors Nov. 20, 1912. (See Minn. H. Soc. Coll. Vol. 15.)

Adkins, F.
Allan, William C,,
Ames, James A.
Beadle, Frank
Bennet, Abner C.
Blondo, Lyman
Bostwick, R. C.
Brown, W., Qm. Sergt.
Clark, W. A., Lieut.
Chambers. Thomas
Carr, Ezra T., Sergt.
Corratt, C.
Crandall, James H.
Cushing, M.
Day, J, W.
Doherty, A.
Douglas, C. H.
Florida, Joel
Friedrich, A. A.
Gemasche, Geo.
Getchell, Alva
Getchell, D. W., Sergt.
Green, John
Gideon, Geo. W.
Hale, J. M.
Ham, C. D.
Handy, DeWitt C.
Handy, Joel
Hanscomb, A. B.
Hawkins, D. C.
Hart, Joseph
Higgins, Judson C
Hoag, A.
Hubbard, R. R.
Huckins, J. W.
Hunter, William
Jacques, Winter

Johnson, C.
Kenna, Sergt. Michael
Kirtz, Fred
Laraway, Albert
Larkins, J. K.
Little, Geo. W.
McConnell, J. C.
McNeill, Neill
Marshall, James
Marshall, Thomas
Mayer, Robert
Merritt, L. W.
Morrison, Geo. H.
Muir, Robert
Murch, J. P.
Perkins, J. H.
Rose, Anson H.
Smith, H. A.
Snell, S. D.
Stone, Edwin
Strout, Capt. Richard
Stubbs, Milton C.
Sweeney, James
Sweesing, Fred
Thompson, N. R.
Tippin, F.
Weeks, N. R.
Wise, A. H.
Wolverton, J. A.
Worthingham, Emory

SCOUTS.

Jesse V. Branham Jr.
Thomas G. Holmes
Albert H. Sperry—all these
of Whitcomb's Company
Albert H. DeLong. a cite
guide for Strout.

Strout's company retreated to Hutchinson, and entered the stockade. The wounded were housed in the hotel adjoining; they were awakened at daybreak by a fusilade of bullets, but all escaped safely to the stockade. The Indians kept up a long range attack during the day. The only casualties were the murders of the Spaude family, recorded before.

BATTLE AT WOOD LAKE.

The battle at Wood Lake, on September 23rd, was the end of the outbreak, so far as fighting by the Indians was concerned.

Knowing that Sibley with his command had started out to capture them, the hostiles resolved to make a desperate effort to stop them. After a very heated council, it was decided to creep on the camp and ambush the command as it started under way in the early morning. A squad from the Third Regt., started with teams to get some potatoes, at a nearby point, and driving across the prairie, ran into the concealed warriors. The fight was on at once, and the ambush defeated. In about two hours they were well whipped, and Little Crow and most of the hostiles were heading for the wild west, never to annoy Minnesota, in numbers, again.

Of the troops, were killed or died from wounds: Matthew Cantwell, Anthony C. Collins, Charles E. Frink, Joseph Pereau, DeGrove Kimball, Richard McElroy and Edwin E. Ross.

Indians killed: Wa-he-canka-maza (Iron Shield), Ta-saka (Hoof rattler), Wa-konza (His law) Marpiya-ho-tanka (Loud voice cloud), Wakan-hdi-xica (Bad lightning), Waxicum-tanka (Big Whiteman) Pa-ji-sku-cinca-cepa (Twin son of sweet grass), Maza -mani (Iron Walker), Tate-yuha-hdi-najin (Comes back with the wind), Cetan-wi-cakte (Hawk that kills), A-han-i-najin (Stands upon), Ai-ya (Talks about things), Maza-wakute (Iron shooter), Chief Maka-to (Blue Earth). The latter attempted to stop a spent cannon ball. Iron Walker attempted to approach the troops with a white rag tied on a stick, but was shot down, either by soldiers or the hostiles, and died in a few hours. He was a friendly, and a good Indian. Undoubtedly, some one had him in mind when the State erected the ridiculous "Mauzo-monee" monument to Friendly Chippewa— at Fort Ridgely. He lost his life following Sibley's directions for friendlies to approach his camp.

THE SIBLEY EXPEDITION OF 1863,

For the purpose of punishing the Indians, and stopping the frontier depredations, on the 16th day of June, 1863, started for the Northwest. Many of the hostiles were hunting buffalo on the prairies, and in the same vicinity was Standing Buffalo (Ta-tanka-najin) with his band. These had remained away during the massacre, and blamed the Lower Indians for the outbreak. A meeting of Sibley and the Indians was to take place, when Little Fish, a member of the notorious Inkpa-duta band, without cause or warning, shot and killed Dr. Joseph S. Weiser, and a general melee followed. Standing Buffalo's band fled to the north, and the others west to the Missouri river. A few of the Indians were killed. Sibley pursued those who went westward, and had a light engagement at several points, but drove the Indians beyond the Missouri river. Two sad incidents were the murders of Lieut. Ambrose Freeman, of St. Cloud, while hunting; and Lieut Beever, of Sibley's staff, waylaid while bearing dispatches. Others killed in this campaign, were: Corps. John Platt and Zenas Blackman, Horatio N. Austin, Wm. H. Chase, Joseph Delaney, Anton Holzen, Ernest Hoffinmaster, David LaPlant, Andrew Moore, Nicholas Miller, Geo. W. Northrup, Theodore Rosch, Gustaf A. Starke. John Murphy was killed by lightning.

WITH THE INDIANS.

A view of the conditions in the Indian camp is a great help to an understanding of massacre events. As before explained, the first murders were by the Rice Creek band, who with Shak-pi's band induced Little Crow's band to join them. They then swept down on the bands of Big Eagle and Good Thunder, just west of the Agency, the latter strongly objecting to the outbreak. Messengers were sent to the bands below, but the attack was not delayed. Wakuta was over-ruled by his braves, Wapa-sha kept away and tried to hold his men, Taopi was of little influence and inactive. The great incentive to the the Indians was loot, particularly horses, and many scattered to the settlements at an early hour—some at Beaver Falls before the murders at the Agency. After the people were disposed of there, the stores were looted and burned, and the intoxicants were rapidly consumed, so that many were drunk. Pans were thrown in the river for targets and a regular shooting contest held. There was much quarreling over making white people prisoners, the violent demanding that all must be killed. Others determined to save their captive friends. More than a score were taken at the Agency.

At night most of the hostiles went into camp at Little Crow's village, and many more prisoners were brought in during the night. Orders were issued to all, to assume the Indian dress, and to form into one camp. Quarreling, drunkenness, over-eating and division of spoils, prevented an attack on the almost helpless fort, or New Ulm, though a slight attack was made on the latter, on Tuesday night. This night Maj. Jos. R. Brown's family of mixed-bloods, with white relatives and friends, came in as captives. The quarrel over captives was violently renewed, but as Mrs. Brown was well-related among the Sissetons, on whose assistance they depended, they were hidden and protected. Chas Blair, the son-in-law was assisted to escape. Mrs. Brown's father Akipa, (meeting), came in a few days and took the family to the Upper Agency. On Thursday, August 28th, Little Crow and the hostiles with their prisoners, moved past the Sisseton camp, and ordered them to follow, which they did for two rea-

sons—to avoid trouble with the hostiles, who far
outnumbered them, and to avoid a position between
the hostiles and whites.

Thirteen friendlies had banded together at the
Upper Agency, and had occupied the government
buildings. As they originated the Friendly camp,
they are named here: Maza-mani (Iron walker) Hin-
ta-chan (Basswood), Shupe-heya (Intestines came
out), Peta-koyag-i-nape (Appeared clothed in fire),
Akipa (Meeting), Charles and Thomas Crawford,
Han-yo-kiya (Flies in the night), Gabriel Renville,
Wican-rpi-nonpa (Two stars), Iniha (Excited) Koda
(Friend) and Rupa-hu (Wing). Crow ordered them
out of the buildings, and they were burned down.
Two camps were made near the Riggs Mission, but
separate. Soon after, about 200 hostiles, came to the
friendlies, and after warlike demonstrations, said:
"We have come for you, and if you do not come,
the next time we will come to attack you." This
angered the friendlies, and they called together all
their people and said: "The Medawakantons have
many white prisoners. Can it be possible that it is
their object to make us their captives too? Call together those who are Wapatons and Sissetons, and
we will prepare to defend ourselves." A "Soldiers
Lodge was formed with Gabriel Renville, Joseph La
Framboise, Marpiya-hdi-nape and Wakpa-i-yu-we-ga
(River crosser), chosen for headmen, and a war
tent erected. The hostiles invited them to a council at which Maza-kute-mani (Shoots as he walks),

also called Little Paul, spoke for the friendlies, ask-
ing for the release of all white prisoners unable to
bear arms.

He was replied to by Wakinyan-to-iciye (Thunder that paints itself blue), opposing the release.
There was much excitement and the council broke
up. A few days later the friendlies again went to
the hostile camp and demanded the return of property taken from mixed-bloods. They were at once
told: "The mixed-bloods should not be alive; they
should have been killed." When Little Paul had
taunted the hostiles with murdering women and
children, and being afraid of the soldiers, some cried
out "kill him." Paul said: "Some of you say kill
me. Bluster away. I am not afraid. I am not a
woman. There are 300 men around me whom you
will have to kill before you have finished." Little
Crow then said: "Paul wants to make peace. It is
impossible to do so if we wanted to. As for me, I
will kill as many of the whites as I can and fight
them till I die. I tell you we must fight and perish
together." After this council the friendly camp was
moved to Red Iron's village. When the hostiles followed, they were stopped by Red Iron's men who
fired their guns as a warning. The hostiles were allowed to camp on promise not to go further on the
Sisseton reservation. Soon after this Taopi, Good
Thunder and His Thunder, with some followers left
the hostiles and joined the friendly camp. Several
times the hostiles made a show of attacking the

camp, but its growing strength, and fear of Sisseton retaliation held them from doing injury.

On Sept. 22d, Little Crow's crier went about the camps, announcing that the soldiers were coming and that all must go to give them battle, under penalty of punishment by the hostiles' Soldiers Lodge. Matters came to a crisis, and finally the friendlies decided to go but privately agreed to stand by while Sibley whipped the hostiles—as they knew he would do. There went down to the point chosen for battle 738 Indians, of which at least one-third were friendlies. Wood Lake battle was fought as described, and confusion reigned supreme. Little Crow told his men to pack up to go to the plains west, and said the captives must be killed first. During the absence of the hostiles at battle, trenches for defense were dug in the friendly camp, and most of the captives secreted there. Those who held captives were anxious to be rid of them when the soldiers came, so went into the friendly camp with them. Crow and about 200 followers fled to the west. Sibley came to the camp on the 24th, and the prisoners were taken to the military camp. There were four white men, and 104 women and children.

The 1,918 Indians and 162 mixed-bloods were kept in camp until October 4th, when most of them and the prisoners were sent down river; the Indians to the Upper Agency where they were put to work harvesting the crops, and the captives to St. Peter. On October 15th, all gathered at the Redwood or

Lower Agency, and three weeks were spent in trials. The uncondemned Indians and families were sent to Fort Snelling on Nov. 9th, and the condemned sent to Mankato. At Mankato on Dec. 26th, 38 were hanged, Round Wind was pardoned, and one died. The Indians sent to Fort Snelling, were poorly cared for and some died, and some of their scanty property was stolen. The following spring all were sent by boat up the Missouri river to the Crow Creek Agency, about 200 miles above Yankton, Dak. Ter. The condemned Indians at Mankato, were sent to a military prison at Davenport, Iowa, from which those who survived were pardoned in 1866. There were only 177 of these to be pardoned at this time; a few had been freed and the balance had died.

From what is given here, and the sources of information are beyond dispute, it will be seen that there were many Lower Indians opposed to the outbreak and its horrors. From August 18th to Sept. 25th, Indian friends protected and fed more than 100 whites—only one (Gustave Kitzman) was killed. And this was in the hostile camp where killing a prisoner would have been on a par with shooting a neighbors' dog, among white people. At the very start the Upper Indians defied the hostiles by saving the lives of the 62 people who John Other Day conducted to Hutchinson, and the Missionary party of some 30 who escaped to Henderson. It is a fact that there was immediate and determined opposition, and warlike organization by the Upper Indians against the hostiles. It took real courage to stand up in council where there were hunreds of savages with loaded guns in their hands, and denounce their conduct. Despite all the good done, all the danger and privation suffered, these Indians were treated with the same severity as the hostiles; robbed of their possessions, and carried off to a wilderness. Though good men and true have ever denounced their treatment in vain, against the politicians and government officials. There has been but one answer: "The only good Indian, is a dead one". No other civilized nation has made slaves of the black race or robbed the red race, but our own.

An item we cannot pass without notice is the loss or concealment of department records in Indian matters. In the Sisseton Claims trials an extensive search for records of the massacre was made, in all departments, even the White house, with the result that a list of the Indians pardoned in 1866, was all that was found. Records of the trials of 38 hanged, 265 imprisoned, etc., are missing. If the trial records in the Minn. Hist. Society are a fair sample of trials of Indians for murder—it is well if decent people never see them.

Narratives by Samuel J. Brown.

LITTLE CROW'S LAST BATTLE.

The day after the battle at Wood Lake, where the Lower Indians intended to wipe out Sibley's army, but were defeated and routed instead, Little Crow returned to his camp crestfallen, saddened and disheartened. Standing outside his teepee, he called his warriors together, and told them to pack up and leave, and save their families; that the troops would soon be upon them and no time should be lost. In the evening Little Crow and about 200 warriors and their families fled toward Devil's Lake. It was from Devil's Lake that Little Crow made his ill-fated trip to the Missouri river. In the early part of Nov. '62 the wily chief planned to go to Fort Berthold, on a peace mission with Gros Ventres, Mandan and Ree tribes, the object being to induce them to join in raids on Minnesota settlers the following spring. Approaching the Mandan village in the usual style of peace-making, among Indians—dancing, whooping and firing of guns, making as much noise as possible while holding aloft and extending the peace pipe, they were fired upon by the Berthold Indians.

The recent killing and scalping of a leading Ree chief and many warriors, (by other Sioux tribes) made the Rees anxious for revenge. They met the peace-makers in a vicious attack. The others had also suffered much from the Sioux and were glad to help their Ree friends; so, Little Crow's men were overwhelmingly out numbered, and were beaten and compelled to flee for their lives. Many were over-taken, slaughtered and scalped. Among these was Xunka-cistina (Little dog), who had warned myself and sister on August 18th, of the outbreak at the Lower Agency. This battle was Little Crow's un-doing. Upon his return, he at once broke camp, and with about 100 men with their families fled to Cana-da. The others scattered to various points among friends. In June 1863 Little Crow and 16 others went to Minnesota on a marauding expedition, and he was killed by the Lamsons near Hutchinson.

In some mysterious manner the Indian prisoners at Fort Snelling knew of Little Crow's defeat, soon after it occurred, and I heard it, and told I. V. D. Heard of it, but he evidently placed no credence in the report. However, while serving as Interpreter at Crow Creek in the summer of 1863 I was placed in charge of an Indian prisoner named Maza-kan (Gun), who had been with Crow, and gave me the details as described.

A DAKOTA SCANDAL AND TRAGEDY.

An interesting story, is that of an affair which

occurred during the removal of the Indians to the Crow Creek reservation in 1863. A practice of the Dakota's was to cut off the ears and nose of women unfaithful to their husbands—suicide usually followed—and this has a bearing on our story. One Te-maza (Gun), became enamored of a young woman, while on the steamer going up the Missouri, and his conduct led to strong objections, and violent tongue-lashings by his wife. He bore it all while the troops were about, but when at last free on the reservation he wreaked vengeance by cutting off her ears and nose, and slashing her face generally. The wife after declaring her innocence of any ill-doings, and calling her friends to avenge her, sought the only relief for a Dakota woman wronged, and committed suicide by hanging. The ire of her family was aroused, and they demanded the death of Te-maza. Col. Martin, the officer in charge, knowing the guilt of the man as being the cause of the suicide, and also that the Indians would surely kill him if the affair was let run, and that probably others would be involved, captured Te-maza and held him for Indian punishment. On the day set for execution, he was foot-bound and placed under a tree. On one side of the ravine troops were drawn up; on the other, the Indians gathered. Te-maza, knowing of the Mankato hanging, evidently expected to be hung. He would look up into the tree, give the war-whoop, and then sing his death-song. Contrary to some very modern notions, this death-song was

not a very musical number; but was a reiteration of
the fact that he was going to death unafraid, that
he had punished many enemies, and that he defied
them one and all. The father-in-law was called up,
given a revolver, and told to shoot the murderer of
his daughter, but he could not handle this and asked
for a gun. This gave time for more war-whoops and
death song. Interpreter Sam Brown was running
about acting as orderly for the Colonel, and was
now included as an enemy. When the gun was secured the father weakened and wanted some one else
to do the shooting; a brother also declined the job.
Te-maza singing his defiance, managed to get near
the father, and quicker than a flash drew a knife he
had concealed and gashed the unsuspecting father
deeply, across the stomach. As he fell Te-maza added a new verse of triumph to his song. Seeing this
botch of affairs, an Indian came up and demanded
that he be allowed to put Te-maza out of his sus-
pense and harmfulness. He was given the gun, and
shot Te-maza through the breast and he fell on his
face. The Colonel started to go up and see if the
man was dead, when Brown shouted a warning that
the man was not dead. He feared the Indian trick
of feigning death and stabbing an enemy. Te-maza
was shot twice more before the body relapsed, and
death was certain. When the body was examined
two more knives were found concealed in the clothing. The execution, crude as it was, satisfied the
Indians and there was no further trouble.

CAPTURE OF THE J. R. BROWN FAMILY.

One of the most interesting events was the capture of the Jos. R. Brown family, (mixed bloods except Blair a son-in-law, and Angus Brown's wife, a McFadden). Mrs. Brown was a daughter of Akipa, a prominent Wapaton, and this probably saved their lives. Nearly all present understood what was said by the Indians, a very unusual occurrence. As the story has been published, only the main facts, as related by Samuel Brown are given:

"On Monday, Aug. 18th, Sister Nellie and I drove to the Upper Agency, from our home some six miles below. On the way Xunka-cistinna (Little dog) stopped us and told that the Lower Indians were killing everybody, and begged us to turn back and tell mother, and get out of the country. This Indian was under many obligations to my father, but was an inveterate liar, so we made our trip and returned home. Father was away; and when we told what we had heard mother was worried, but the others treated the matter lightly. About 4 o'clock next morning I heard some one calling, and when Blair called out "What do you want, this time of night?" Old Peter Rouilliard, a Frenchman who had long lived with the Indians, shouted "For God's sake hurry; the Indians are killing everybody at the Agency. I have barely escaped with my life." We prepared for flight at once, with three wagons and ox teams. By the time we were ready several of the neighbors had arrived—two Ingalls girls, Charles Holmes, Leopold Wohler and wife, Garvie's cook and some I do not recall; there were 26 in our party— we started for Fort Ridgely, on the road along the north side of the river. When we had gone about six miles we saw some people at the right of us, and they began to run toward the road ahead. Soon an Indian on horseback popped up before us and beckoned the others, who soon surrounded us.

Mother grasped the situation—they were the murdering Indians. She hoped to save us by making herself known. So she stood stood up in the wagon and waving her shawl cried out that she was a Sisseton, a relative of Waanatan, Scarlet Plume, Akipa, and was the friend of Standing Buffalo. She demanded their protection. Many Indians gathered about us, some with blackened faces and bloody hands demanding that we be killed. The vicious Cut Nose Shak-pi and Dowaniye (Singer), came up flourishing their tomahawks in our faces, singing the war song:

> "Ai-xica canze mea ca-e
> Niyake bawa-hunhun we."

Which is: "The Dutchmen (bad talkers) have made me so angry I will butcher them alive," "Dutchman" was a term of reproach applied to all who lived or dressed as white men. There happened to be one in the crowd who had come to our house in a freezing condition, and mother had taken him in and cared for him. He came running to us with murderous in-

tentions, but recognizing mother he mounted the
wagon, and telling his experience, declared that he
would protect us with his life.   After he had spoken,
the Indians went aside and conferred.   On returning
they declared the white men must be killed; they did
not dare save them, as their own lives would be in
danger from the Soldiers Lodge.   Mother pleaded,
argued and threatened to save all, for she knew if
killing commenced, there would be no control of the
bloodthirsty Indians.   Cut Nose cried out: "Save
them! save them!   Are you not grateful that your
own life is saved."   Mother said: "Remember what
I say—if you harm any of these you will have to
answer to the whole Sisseton and Wapaton tribe."
After much bitter wrangling they ordered Lonsman
to drive the oxen, Holmes, Wohler, Garvies cook and
one other were ordered to leave across the prairie to
the north, and Rouilliard to go back to his Indian
wife.   The rest of us were to be taken to the hostile
camp for disposal.   We were taken to Rice Creek,
and finally to Crow's camp, fearing every minute for
our lives.   Little Crow, aside from his friendship
for us, better understood the seriousness of mother's
argument, he desired Sisseton aid, and he feared to
arouse their anger.   We were cared for and protected in his house.   Fearing for Blair's safety he was
aided to escape.   Being far from a strong man, he
never recovered from the exhaustion and exposure
but died at Henderson the following spring.   Lonsman made his escape.   Akipa came in a few days

and took our family to the Upper Agency. The rest were held as prisoners. Mother saved the entire party by her energetic action; all lived to see peace and order restored. Those left in the hands of the hostiles were at Camp Release.

DEATH OF LITTLE CROW.

Related by J. B. Lamson.

In the early summer of 1863 most of the settlers about Hutchinson were living near the stockade, as a company of soldiers was stationed there. Some of the settlers were cultivating their farms, but their families remained in town. I had spent a part of the time on the homestead six miles north of the village, caring for the stock and crops. On the 3rd of July I went to the village, to spend the Fourth, and father and brother Chauncey took my place. That evening, about an hour before sundown, while hunting deer near Scattered Lakes, they came to an open space in the woods filled by brush and a raspberry patch. They had walked some distance into the opening, on the road, when suddenly they observed an Indian jumping over his pony, and another larger Indian standing by. Providentially, the Indians had not observed them, and they immediately sought cover in the bushes, and made their plans; for to see an Indian meant death to him or his white enemy, in those days.

My father, Nathan, was past 63 years old, but was a true frontiersman, and Chauncey had profited

by his training. Chauncey took a position covering
the road between them and the Indians, and stayed
ready with cocked rifle while father crept forward
concealing himself behind a spreading poplar tree.
Through the leaves of the tree he shot the the larger
Indian, the ball entering the left groin.   Both the
Indians and father went to the ground, and all was
quiet as death, while each was trying to locate the
other.   Knowing that the powder-smoke would soon
reveal his location, he crawled back in his own path,
and he had scarcely gone two rods when the tree
was riddled with buckshot.   One buckshot struck
him on the shoulder making a slight wound.   He
then turned to the right to get out of the line of fire,
and tried to load his rifle, but got a bullet which was
too large and it stuck when about five inches down
the barrel, and lying down he could not force it further.   He also removed his white shirt, to prevent
discovery, and crawling to the road he crossed it
and hid in a clump of hazel brush.

Little Crow skulked around the raspberry patch
in the road.   As he came in range, Chauncey saw
him and rose to his feet and fired.   Little Crow shot
at the same instant; father did not hear the crack of
Chauncey's rifle in the roar of Little Crow's shot-
gun.   Little Crow shot from the left shoulder, but
evidently did not get the butt at the shoulder before
shooting; the slug from his gun just grazed Chauncey's head.   The ball from Chauncey's rifle struck
the stock of Crow's gun a glancing blow and then

entered his left breast.   Both dropped to the ground.
Chauncey trying to reload his rifle found he had no
bullets; father had put them all in his pocket on
starting out, and this accounts for the ball getting
stuck in his gun—the rifles were of different caliber.
Being thus unarmed, and not knowing how many Indians there might be Chauncey did not dare approach
father, whom he had seen crawl across the road.   He
determined on a ruse to draw the Indians away if
possible, and crawling back a ways rose up in sight
and ran toward Hutchinson.   Father could not see
from his hiding, and did not know the result of the
shooting, but he could hear the Indian groaning, not
ten feet away.   After a time Crow's son Wo-wi-nape
(One who appeareth) came up, and they talked for
some time before the chief died.   When the conver-
sation ceased, and father heard the pony ridden off,
he crept away and came into Hutchinson in the early
morning.   Meantime a party of soldiers and citizens
had gone to our farm where they waited for day light
As I was acquainted with the locality, I was leading
way, and I will never forget the sensation when we
saw a body in the road ahead of us.   That it was
father, seemed to possess me—but I soon saw it was
an Indian.   We could not find father, or any more
Indians, so we took up the trail of the pony, but we
were overtaken by troopers scouting for Indians, so
we turned back.   While we were gone father and a
neighbor had come for the body.   They found that
some one had taken the scalp; probably to get the
reward offered by the state for Sioux scalps.

Among those seeing the body, was Hiram Cummins of Co. E, 9th Regt., who declared the body to that of Little Crow.   When his statement was ridiculed he said: "There is no doubt about it.   Here are marks that no man can mistake.   He has double teeth clear around, and both of his wrists are broken and poorly set".   Many could not believe that so inglorious an end had come to Ta-oyate-duta (His scarlet people), war chief of the Medawakantons.

Prisoners Surrendered at Camp Release.
Friday, September 26th, 1862.

1   Adams, Mrs. Hattie (John), captured near Hutchinson.

2   Brown, Mrs. Angus, captured with the Joseph R. Brown family.

3   Busse, Wilhelmina, daughter of Gotttried, captured at Middle Creek, aged 12 years.

4   Busse, Amelia, sister to above aged 7 years.

5   Busse, August, brother aged 14 years.

6   Burns, Mrs. Sarah, captured at Lower Agency.

7   "   child of above.

8   "   same

9   "   same

10   Butler. M. A.   No information.

11   Buhrman, Tobet, aged 18 years, captured at Lower Agency—probably daughter of Baptiste.

12   Carrothers, Mrs. David, captured at Beaver Creek.

13   Infant of above.

14   Clausen, Martha. Mrs Fredrick, Captured near Birch Coulie.

15 Infant daughter of above.

16 Same.

17 Cardenelle, Mrs. Margaret, captured at Birch Coulie.

18 Child of same.

19 Consalle, Nancy, 8 years old, captured at Lower Agency.

20 Consalle, Philomena, 4 years, sister to above.

21 Earle, Mrs. J. W. Earle, at Beaver Creek.

22 " Julia, 13 years, daughter.

23 " Elmira, 7 years, daughter.

24 Eisenreich. Mrs. Balthasar, at Beaver Cceek.

25 " Peter.

26 " Sophie.

27 " Mary.

28 " Joseph.

29 Frass, Justina. wife of August, at Sacred Heart.

30 " child.

31 " child.

32 Gluth, August, 14 years. No information.

33 Huggins, Sophia J., wife of Amos W., captured at Lac qui Parle.

34 Huggins, Charles.

35 " Lettie, infant.

36 Inefeldt, Minnie, wife of Wm.. Beaver twp.

37 " Infant.

38 Ingalls. Amanda, dtr J. H., aged 14, captured with Brown family.

39 Ingalls, Jennie, aged 12, sister.

40 Juni, Benedict, Jr., aged 14, La Croix Creek.

41 Kitzman, Louis, aged 14, son of Paul, captured at Sacred Heart.

42 Krieger, Henrietta, aged 3, daughter of Fredrick, captured at Sacred Heart.

43 Koch, Mrs. Augusta, wife of Andrew, captured at Lake Shetek.

44   Krause, Dorothea, wife of T., at Sacred Heart.
45   "   child.
46   "   child.
47   "   Pauline, sister of T. Krause.
48   Laramie, Mrs. Mary, captured at Sacred Heart.
49   "   Louisa, 18 years.
50   "   Edward, 15 years.
51   Lammers, Mrs. Sophia, wife of William, captured
at Sacred Heart.
52 Lammers, Fred, 7 years.
53   "   Charles, an infant.
54   Lenz, Augusta, daughter of Ernest, captured at
Middle Creek.
55   Launt, Mrs. Susie, captured at Lower Agency.
56   "   child of above.
57   LaBlaugh, Mrs. Antoine, at Lower Agency.
58   ',   child.
59   "   child.
60   Lange, Mrs. Amelia, probably Middle Creek.
61   "   Child.   .
62   "   Child.
63   LaBelle, Louis, near Upper Agency.
64   McLane, Mrs. Rosalie, at Upper Agency.
65   "   child.
66   "   ehild.
67   Nichols, Henrietta, aged 12.   No information.
68   Patterson, Mrs. Mary, near Madelia.
69   "   Antoine.
70   "   Peter.
71   Piquar, Elizabeth, young daughter of Eusebius, at
Birch Coulie,
72   Record, Elizabeth, 3 years, niece Mrs. Cardenelle.
73   Roseyuse, Mrs., at Upper Agency.
74   Renville, Mrs. J., wife of a mixed-blood.
75   Rousseau, Peter, Upper Agency.
76   Rouilliard, Peter, Upper Agency,

77 Schmidt, Minnie, 4 years, at Middle Creek. Died at Fort Ridgely in a few days.

78 Schwandt, Mary E., near Fort Ridgely with the Patoille party. Home Middle Creek.

79 Spencer, George, at Lower Agency.

80 Thompson, George, 18 years, Lower Agency.

81 Urban, Mrs. John, at Sacred Heart.

82 "   Ernestine.

83 "   Rose

84 "   Louise.

85 "   Albert.

86 Valiant, Mrs. Harriet, at Lower Agency.

87 "   child.

88 "   child.

89 Vanasse, Mrs. Matilda, near Fort Ridgely.

90 "   child.

91 "   child.

92 Williams, Miss Mattie, with Patoille party.

93 Woodbury, Mrs. Mary, at Lower Agency.

94 "   child.

95 "   child.

96 "   child.

97 "   child.

98 Wright, John, 3 years old, at Lake Shetek.

99 Wakefield, Mrs. Sarah, wife of Dr. J. B., Upper Agency physician, captured near Redwood river.

100 Wakefield, James, 6 years old.

101 "   Nellie, infant.

102 White, Urania S., wife of N. D., Beaver Creek.

103 "   Julia, aged 14 yeors.

104 "   Frank, infant.

105 Wohler, Frances, wife of Leopold, Brown family.

106 Wilson, Eunice, 18 years, Lower Agency.

107 Yess, Henrietta, 3 years, daughter of Michael, at Sacred Heart Creek.

In addition to the above there were 162 mixed-bloods whom the hostiles claimed as captives.

Tonwan-ite-ton (Face of the village), baptized as Lorenzo Lawrence, secretly took from the camp Mrs. J. W. DeCamp and her two children and took them to Fort, by canoe. On the way he picked up Mrs. Magloire Robideaux, and five children, mixed-bloods who escaped from the hostile camp.

Anawang-mani(Hobbles along), baptized as Simon, took a Mrs. Neuman and her three children to the fort from the hostile camp, in his cart.

Mrs. Wm. L. Quinn, and her children Ellen, William and Thomas, her mother Mrs. Elizabeth Jeffries, Mrs. Philander Prescott and daughter Julia, all mixed-bloods, escaped during the Wood Lake battle and got to the fort safely.

Dakota Indians Hung at Mankato.

Friday, December 26th, 1862.

1 Tipi-hdo-niche.—Forbids his dwelling
2 Wyata-tonwan—His people
3 Taju xa—Red otter
4 Hinhan shoon koyag mani—Walks clothed in an owl's tail.
5 Maza bomidu—Iron blower
6 Wapa duta—Scarlet leaf
7 Wahena—(Meaning unknown)
8 Sna mani—Tinkling walker
9 Rda inyanke—Rattling runner
10 Dowan niye—The singer
11 Xunka ska—White dog
12 Hepan—Family name for second son
13 Tunkan icha ta mani—Walks with his grandfather
14 Ite duta—Scarlet face
15 Amdacha—Broken to pieces.

16 Hepidan—Family name for third son.
17 Marpiya te najin—Stands on a cloud　(Cut nose)
18 Henry Milord—(French mixed-blood)
19 Chaska dan—Family name for 1st son—dan little)
20 Baptiste Campbell—(French mixed blood)
21 Tate kage—Wind maker
22 Hapinkpa—Tip of the horn
23 Hypolite Auge—(French mixed-blood)
24 Nape shuha—Does not flee
25 Wakan tanka—Great Spirit
26 Tunkan koyag i najin—Stands clothed with his grandfather
27 Maka te najin—Stands upon earth
28 Pazi kuta mani—Walks prepared to shoot
29 Tate hdo dan—Wind comes back
30 Waxicun na—Little Whiteman
31 Aichaga—To grow upon
32 Ho tan inku—Voice heard in returning.
33 Cetan hunka—The parent hawk
34 Hda hin hda—To make a rattling noise
35 Chanka hdo—Near the woods
36 Oyate tonwan—The coming people
37 Mehu we mea—He comes for me
38 Wakinyan na—Little thunder

In addition to this list, two others were named to be hung—Tate mima, (Round wind) who was pardoned; one report says one died; one that Godfrey, whose sentence was commuted, was of the 40to be hung.

There is no question that several of these were unjustly executed, as No. 21, a half-witted son of Wakan mani, (Spirit walker), aged 14 years.　He was present at the murder of Amos Huggins, at Lac qui Parle, but did not assist　Ta-in-na (Leather blanket) and Ho si di (He brought the news) committed the murder, they escaped with Little Crow.　Xunka ska, No. 11, (White dog), did the talking at Redwood Ferry; neither White men or Indians agree on what he said; he was under duress, and had up to that time been a 'man with good reputation. Waxicun-na No. 30, a young boy, not very intelligent, answered to the name of another man, and was put in the death-pen. Chaska-dan No. 19, was hung for the murder of Geo. Gleason; Mrs. Wakefield, the only witness, swore to his innocence, made every effort to save him, and later published a pamphlet denouncing the execution and officials,

These incidents are not given to palliate the offences of the Indians, nor to malign the commission, but rather to show the abuses of the Indians in the treatment given them. In the trials Justice was not only blind but ignorant, and the officials faced an enraged public. Read the trial proceedings at the Historical Society if you doubt the criticism.

John Campbell, a son of Scott Campbell the interpreter at Fort Snelling in early years, brother of Baptiste No. 20, was hung at Mankato by an impromptu court on May 3, 1865. He had participated in the murder of the Jewett family, in Rapidan township.

Chief Shak-pi, (Little six), and Pejuhuta-tha (Medicine Bottle), were captured by Hatch's Battalion, and hanged at Fort Snelling in 1865.

Indians Pardoned at Davenport, Iowa.

January 20th, 1866.

In this list are names of 177 of the 303 Indians condemned by the military Court, all of whom were sentenced to be hung except Nos. 6, 37, 61 and 170—first three to 5 years, the last to 10 years. It is probable that about one-third of those imprisoned had died.

Credit for the translation is largely due to Samuel J. Brown, whose acquaintance with, and knowledge of these men made it possible to decipher the muddled up government record. Even to him, 14 names are meaningless.

In the spelling of these names, "a" is given the sound of "ah", E as long a, I as long e, J as zh, and X as sh. For instance Maza-xa—Mah-zah-shah.

No. Age   Name   Meaning
 1 50 years old. Napinkpa-rota "Gray mittens".
 2 32 Toruivanwakinyan. (This name is from the Gov't record and is meaningless).
 3 23 Otiruyapa. Meaningless.
 4 25 Ta-Marpiya-rota. "His gray cloud".
 5 24 Wanna. "Now".
 6 30 Tukan-gi. "Brown [rusty] sacred stone".
 7 18 Agu-yanna. Causes to scorch.
 8 34 Marpiya-tanka. Big cloud.
 9 21 Tukan-wakan. Mysterious or sacred stone.
10 27 Sagyekiton. Wears a cane.
11 23 Tate-ohomni-inyanke. Runs around the wind.
12 28 Tukan-to-iciye. Sacred stone that paints itself blue.

48 41 Wasu-wakanhdi. Lightning hail.
49 24 Patecage. [Meaningless]
50 23 Nom-ahdi. Brings back two.
51 20 Kohdamni. Headed off standing.
52 29 Kieos-mani. Beckons as he walks.
53 29 Rewanke. Frost.
54 52 Akicita-wakan. Sacred soldier.
55 40 Waxtexte. Many of a good kind.
56 23 Tuwan-okawinge-dan. Surrounds (or circles) with his eyes open.
57 36 Waxicun-sapa. Black whiteman—Negro.
58 41 Acaxin. Steps over.
59 24 Oran-wan-yakapi' They see his actions.
60 32 Ta-canrpi-iyojanjanna. His bright tomahawk.
61 24 Yu-snasna. Makes a ring or tinkle.
62 21 Anpetu-ojanjanna. Bright day—sunshiny.
63 21 Iwankab-najin. Stands above—or over.
64 33 Marpiya-cokaya-mani. Walks in cent'r of clds
65 34 Pa-tain. Head appears.
66 32 Marpiya-duta. Scarlet or red cloud.
67 30 Nina-iyopta. Goes ahead very swiftly.
68 32 Onktomi-ska. White spider.
69 38 Maka-nahoton-mani. Treads the earth with a loud noise as he walks.
70 36 Tate-wakanhdi-kagedan. Makes wind out of lightning.
71 24 Maka-ohomni-kudan. Comes back around the earth
72 38 Maka-a-inyanke. Runs upon earth.
73 47 Taninyan-ku. Returns appearing.
74 28 Maza-ixkad-mani. Walks along as he plays with iron.
75 31 Marpiya-iduhomni. The cloud turns itself around.
76 37 Bu-ku-dan. Returns with a loud noise.
77 35 Wakinyan-gi. Rusty or brownish cloud.
78 26 Cetan-rota. Gray hawk.

13	35	Tawanruchawazte. [Meaningless].
14	32	Rmun-yanku. Returns with a buzz.
15	40	Wapa-rota. Gray leaf.
16	47	Tatetuyayedan. [Meaningless].
17	32	Tatoheya. Against the wind—or current.
18	17	Han-wakan-hdi. Night lightning.
19	45	Wahorpi. Nest.
20	34	Maza-wakinyan-na. Iron thunder.
21	28	Maza-iheyedan. Thrusts at iron.'
22	38	Maza-nabdezedan. Bursts iron with his feet.
23	32	Taniyan-hdi-najin. Stands fast.
24	45	Karboka. Sailing—or floating.
25	41	Marpiya-akicita. Cloud Soldier.
26	28	Pawaktedan. [Meaningless].
27	39	Pejuhuta-ska. White medicine.
28	35	Wajuhutka-sapa. Black bird is yellow.
29	40	Ta-canrpi-tanka. His big tomahawk.
30	30	Waxicun-ixnana. Lone whiteman.
31	22	Tukan-aputag-mani. Presses the sacred stone with his hands while walking.
32	23	Anpao-hdi-najin. Returns and stands at daybreak.
33	23	Wakan-dowan. Sings sacredly.
34	23	Wakan-na. Sacredly,
35	17	Marpiya-topa-dan. Four clouds.
36	31	Marpiya-coka. In middle, or amidst, clouds.
37	22	Marpiya-ota. Many clouds.
38	20	Tawa-hinkpe. His arrow.
39	38	Huntka. Cormorant.
40	28	Maza-yuha-mani. Carries iron as he walks.
41	25	Tawa-hinkpe-duta. His scarlet arrow.
42	33	Oceti-duta. Place of scarlet fire.
43	42	Marpiya-hepiya. Lowering clouds.
44	34	Taxina-wakan-hdi. His lightning blanket.
45	38	Cetan-rota. Gray hawk.
46	26	Pearape. [Meaningless].
47	23	Tate-yuha-mani. Carries the wind as he walks

79 40 Ite-wakanhdi-ota. Many lightnings (forked) in face

80 24 Tacanrpi-wakanna. His mysterious, or sacred tomahawk

81 38 Woteca. Wild animal

82 41 Tawa-hinkpe-ota. His many arrows

83 31 Maza-iciyapa. Irons striking together

84 28 Anpao-hiyaye. Passes at daybreak

85 40 Iyotan-ona. Shoots more than others

86 33 Tacan-dupa. His pipe.

87 26 Maza-koyag-i-nape. Appears clothed in iron

88 70 Wakan-tapi. Sacred liver—digestive organ

89 24 Tate-canxicedan. Lonesome wind

90 23 Ehake-o-najin. Amongst the last to stand

91 46 Ie-wakan. Sacred talker

92 53 Wicartake. Comes near touching

93 34 Neapowamriyamne. Meaningless

94 36 Hu-patin. Stiff legged

95 65 Hocoka. Middle or center, of camp

96 50 Maka-nartake, Kicks the earth

97 30 Wakanhdi-rota. Gray lightning.

98 38 Okaze. Skates, or slides

99 25 Waxicun-Ie. Talks whiteman.

100 34 Tuwan-najidan. Stands looking

101 57 Nagi-car-mani. Ghost that walks on ice.

102 18 Ta-hanpe-xica. His bad moccasin.

103 24 Maza-a-inyanke. He makes iron to run

104 34 Cannope-sa. Smokes much.

105 23 Hepan. Family name for second-born, if a son

106 26 Maza-nahoton. Presses iron with his feet making it to bellow

107 27 Otin-iyapa. Strikes together with a noise.

108 56 Taxaduta. Meaningless

109 25 Magasan. Swan

110 57 Tate-hdi-najin. Wind returns standing.

111 25 Wan-wakan-kida. Believes his arrows sacred

112 37 Marpiya-Waxicun. Cloud whiteman.

113 56 Tio-duta. Scarlet teepee, or tent.
114 23 Marpiya-xotedan. Smoky cloud.
115 25 Tukan-xa-iciye Sacred stone paints itself red.
116 60 Ti-nazipe. His bow.
117 40 Ehna-mani. Walks amongst.
118 25 Wamdi-wanyakapi. Eagles see him.
119 37 Cotanka-maza. Iron flute
120 64 Caske-pte-dan. Chaska—first-born son
121 47 Oeixanjidan. Meaningless
122 30 Hepi-pte-cedan. Hapan—third born son.
123 61 Xunkardo. Dog growls
124 56 Kaya. Carries for another
125 42 Wakanyan-kute. Shoots sacredly
126 41 Hinhan-duta. Scarlet owl
127 64 Wakanhdi-kudan. Lightning comes back
128 56 Ta-sagye Maza. His Iron cane
129 56 Anpetu-iyokihe. Next to day
130 40 Hoka-gopa. Snoring herou
131 47 Tatanka-cistinna. Little buffalo
132 47 Marpiya-owanca. Clouds all around
133 34 Keawonge. Meaningless
134 69 Maza-wamnuha. Iron gourd
135 34 Ti-okiti. Occupies his own tent .
136 29 Wazi-duta. Scarlet (red) cedar
137 46 Heraka-maza. Iron Elk—if a male
138 30 Painyanke-duta. The scarlet hoop game :
139 30 Taniya-na. Little breath
140 54 Tipi-tawa. His own tent.
141 47 Maka-amani-waxicun. Whiteman walks upon the earth
142 63 Hepan-duta. Scarlet Hepan—2d born son
143 23 Wasu-ratka. Rough hail.
144 50 Wakanyan-najin. Stands sacredly
145 38 Kadutedan. Fanning
146   (See No. 12)
147 34 Tate-peta. Fire wind--wind that burns

148   42   (See No. 14)
149   23   Xa-iciye. Paints himself red
150   24   Maza-wicaxta. Iron man.
151   37   Peji-rota. Gray grass—wild sage
152   70   Ota-dan. Many
153   37   Nagi-kuwa-mani. Chases ghosts as he walks
154   30   Wakan-ideya-mani. Sets fire mysteriously as
                 he walks
155   51   Tate-tokeca. Different kinds of wind
156   36   Wicarca-maza. Old man that is iron
157   58   Napi-xtan. Bother
158   41   Ojanjanna. Bright—sunny
159   34   Marpiya-gidan. Rusty, or brownish, cloud
160   33   Tukan-waxtexte. Good sacred stones
161   37   Sitomni. Everywhere—all around
162   38   Zitkadan-to. Bluebird
163   78   Ta-wo-ta-he duta. His scarlet medicine bag.
164   35   Tinazipe-ojanjan. His shining bow
165   24   Noeive. Meaningless
166   34   Wicanrpi-ota. Many stars
167   25   Wijutita. Meaningless
168   20   Xake-hanske. Long claws.
169   48   Iparte. Bridle or halter
170   29   Joseph Godfrey, a Negro
171   30   Wa-akan inajin. Stands on top (of anything)
172   29   Antoine Provencalle. A mixed blood.
173   38   Tukan-gi-dan. Rusty, or brownish, stone.
174   15   Naguintiankudan. Meaningless
175   15   Hepidan. Third born son.
176   16   Marpiya-wakan-kida. Thinks his cloud sacred
177   24   Louis LaBelle. A mixed blood

List of Refugees at Fort Ridgely.

The following is the Report of the Adjutant General, and is corrected as to names, especially as to spelling, and location. Why other persons known to have been present, are not named, we cannot understand.

Anderson, John, aged 49, home at West Newton.

Bell, Elizabeth, 38 yrs, home at Kasota, husband Chas. R., soldier, killed at Redwood Ferry battle. Her children: Girls M. C. 16. S. M. 14; boy B. M. 12: girls M. E. 8, E. 6; boy C. R. 4; girl M. F. 2 yrs.

Buehro, N, 33, home near fort, wife Anna 30, children daughter W. 5, infant E. year old.

Buehro, A, 32, wife of John killed in Birch Coule twp. H. Buehro, boy, 13 months old.

Betzel. V., aged 19, employed at Agency mess house.

Brunelle, Edward, 35, home at Redwood.

Buhrman, Baptiste 45 yrs, Lower Agency. Wife Susan aged 32 years.

Boelter, Michael. 31 yrs, Middle Creek. Wife and three children killed.

Bjorkman, Petrus, 41 yrs, home St. Paul.

Brisbin, L. P., 47, home Lower Agency. Elizabeth 37, Antoine 10, Louis 8 and Margaret 6 yrs.

Boelter, Julius, 6 months, son of John killed at Middle Creek home.

Comro, J., 37, home LaCroix Creek. Wife May 32 yrs, son W. 6, dtr L. 3. F. an infant.

Chassie, John, 46. R. wife 42, home Beaver Creek.

Clausen, Mrs. Charles, 57, Birch Coulie, husband and son Frederick killed; son John, 28, with her.

Clock, C. 25, Agency mess house employee.

Dunn, M. E., 27, home Greenleaf, children H. A. 8 yrs, M. B. 7, W. A., 3 years.

Depolder, H., 40. West Newton, wife O., 44 yrs.

Donahue, Dennis, 38, Monny, 28, wife, son James 5. dtr Francis 2, infant daughter.

Dickinson, E., 30, wife of J. C., mess house keeper at Agency; dtr A. 4, son C. 1 year

Dalssy, Herbert, 30 yrs, Lower Agency.

Emery, William, 24, Lower Agency.

Erfkamp, Henry, 29, West Newton.

Froscap, Mary, 65, widow, LaCroix Creek. Eliza 18.

Falteen, John, 35, West Newton.

Horan, Mrs. M. A., 23, Lowell; Minnie E., 4: Walter C. 3; dtr E. R. 1 yr.

Humphrey, John A. 12, son of Philander P., the Agency Physician. Parents, brother and sister killed.

Holveson, John. 35, 4 miles above Redwood, Ellen 35, wife: Thomas 4, dtr G. 2, Martin 6 months.

Hayden, Margaret 19. Beaver Creek, Catherine 1 year. Husband Patrick killed.

Horan, Koran, 37, 8 miles above West Newton; Bridget 24, wife; Millie 3 yrs, 8 months infant.

Hinman, Rev. S. D.. 23, Rector at Agency.

Hewett, C. B., 23. Lower Agency.

Halter, Mrs. S., 45, soldiers' wife; C. son 8 years.

Hoyfron, Patrick C., 35, West Newton. Mary A. 23, wife.

Hamm, Conrad, 25, 8 miles above Redwood.

Hose, John, 25, Lower Agency.

Haley, William, 48, West Newton.

Jones, M., 47, wounded, LaFayette.

Jones, M., 28, wife of Sergt. at fort; son G. W. 6, E. L. daughter 2 years.

Kelly, Catherine, 26,soldiers' wife; Margaret 3 years. Jones, 3 months. Home West Newton.

Kaertner, H. 28, LaCroix Cr'k. Husband Henry killed

Kochendorfer, John, 11, sisters R. 9, K. 7, M. 5.

Krause, T. 32. Sacred Heart. Family prisoners.

Krieger, (Properly Lehn]. Gottlieb, 11, John 9, Sacred Heart. Stepsons of Fredrick Krieger.

Klaron, Peter, 29, 3 miles below Agency.

Lettou, Ann, 42, wife of John killed at the Middle Creek home; sons F. 12, A. 10, August 5, W. an infant.

Lenz, Ernest, 45, Middle Creek, wife W. 42, dtr A 11 dtr L. 6, son H. 1 yr.

Lenz, T., 45, Middle Creek, wife F. 43 years,

Levant, A., 11 years, Beaver Creek.

LaFrambois, Wm.,[13, 4 miles above Redwood. Justine 13, Eliza 7 years.

LaCroix, Louis, 55, LaCroix Creek, Rosette 25, Louis 12, L. 10, Spencer 8, Adrienne 7, Olivia infant.

Laffinmaker, 60, West Newton, Charles 40, Hannah 12, Laura 12.

McAllister, Juliette, 23, soldier husband Henry killed at Ferry battle, girls E. A. 6, L., 3 years.

McConnell, Ellen, 70, LaCroix Creek; Doren 40, and Joseph 25 years.

Magner, John, 35, 4 miles below Agency; wife Nancy 32, James 15, Ann 13, Thomas 12, David 9, Ellen 7. Catherine 4 years,

Magner. Julia, 36, wife of Edward killed at home, four miles below Agency; Margaret 16, James 14, Ellen 9, Mary 5, Patrick 3, David 1 year.

Machansky, Mary, 28, near fort, M. 7, Joe 5, Anthony four months.

Martelle, Oliver, 43, Lower Agency; wife M. 24 yrs.

Mannweiler, C. 23, Middle Creek, wife Gottlieb, killed.

Meyer, John J., 35, Beaver Creek; wife and three children taken prisoners.

Nairn, John, 33, Agency. wife M. 34. dtr C. 10, son J. 6, dtr M. R. 3, son M. J. infant.

O'Thoy, Dennis, 27, 4 miles above West Newton.

Parsley, R. A., 22, soldier husband John, killed at the
    ferry battle.   M. E. an infant.

Perry, Geo. 37, LaCroix Creek; wife Sally 34, dtrs C.
    14, M. 12. Emily 4, Mary 3, Martha, infant; son
    George 6.

Peterson, Alex., 27, below Agency; wife Julia, 22, son
    P. 3, dtr J. infant.

Pereau. E., 33, LaCroix Creek, wife of Peter, killed at
    the home.   Dtrs J. 12,M. 9, F. 5; sons R. 10, Geo 8.

Piquar, Elizabeth, 22, LaCroix Creek, husband Euse-
    bius, killed.   Sons Eusebius 6, C. 1 year.

Reynolds, J. B. 43, Redwood; wife Valencia J. 35 yrs

Robinson, John 51, James 45, West Newton.

Reyff, Emanuel 12, Mary 10, Middle Creek.

Robert, Louis, 51. Agency Trader.

Reed, George, 38, St. Paul.

Roseyuse, —— 26, Yellow Med.; wife taken prisoner.

Sloan, Catherine, 20, Chatfield.

Schilling, E. 16, girl, Fort Ridgely.

Schmal, J. 45, Ft. Ridgely; wife R. 35, dtrs J. 7, M. 6,
    S. 4; sons A. 3, H. 18 months.

Smith, Ellen, 38, moving to Birch Coulie, her husband
    Thomas, killed; Millard 12, John 10. Mary E. 5.

Sier, B. 52, Faribault.

Samson, Anna, 34, moving, Ole husb'd killed; Sam inf't

Smith, H. 38, wife S. N. 37, Agency, dtr N. C. 12.

Stafford, Augustus, 42, West Newton.

Senc, Peter, 35, 8 miles above Redwood.

Sherou, Louis, 40, 4 miles above Redwood, wlfe Jane
    41, dtr Winona 17, sons Frank 3, Louis 2 years.

Schlumberger, Christ., 26, 3 miles above fort.

Thompson, Jones, 57, Redwood.

Whipple, J. C., 39, Faribault.

West, Emily J., 52, Agency.

Witt, Carl 45, LaCroix Creek, wife killed, dtrs L. 9,
    M. 4, sons Wm. 14, C. 7, A. 1 year.

Yess, Michael, 45, wife C. 48 Sacred Heart Crk, August
 14 years. Henrietta 3 yrs taken prisoner.
Zimmermann, Mary 44, blind, Beaver Creek; dts M, 17
 Elizabeth 14; Sam 7. John, husband, and sons
 John and Gottlieb killed at LaCroix Creek.

Indians Killed During Outbreak.

1 To-wa-to. All blue, at Redwood Ferry.
2 Upi-hdi-ga. Striped wing feather, at Ft. Ridgely.
3 Horpi-maza. Iron nest at Ft. Ridgely.
4 Ho-tonna. Animal's voice, at Birch Coulie.
5 Wan-iheya. Shoots the arrow, at Birch Coulie.
6 Ma-tata-ma-hucha. Lean bear, near Lake Shetek.
 At Wood Lake battle:
7 He-i-pa-kan-mani. Rubs his horns against some-
 thing as he walks.
8 Ta--sa-ka. Hoof Rattler.
9 Wa-kon-za. His law.
10 Wakan-hdi-xica. Bad Lightning.
11 A-han-zi. Shade (or shadow).
12 Peji-sku-cinca-cepa. Twin sons of sweet grass.
13 Waxicun-tanka. Big Whiteman.
14 Marpiya-ho-tanka. Loud voice cloud.
15 Wa-ha-canka-maza. His iron shield.
16 Maka-a-mani-wasicun-cinca. Son of whiteman that
 walks on the earth.
17 A-han-i-najin. He stands upon.
18 Cetan-wicakte. Hawk that kills.
19 Ie-ya. Talks about things.
20 Tate-yuha-hdi najin. Comes back standing on the
 wind.
21 Maza-wa-kute. Iron shooter.
22 Maka-to. Blue earth.
23 Maza-mani. Iron walker.

24 Infant, killed by mob at Henderson.
25 Cinkpa. Treetops, at New Ulm.
26 LeBlanc. or Provencalle, at New Ulm.
    At Fort Abercrombie:—
√27 Mato-sapa. Black bear.
28 Sna-sna-mani. Jingling walker.
39 Pi-zona. (Name of a society, or organization.)
30 (Unnamed.) Neighborhood of Acton.

It is probable that Sibley forces killed some four or five of Standing Buffalo's band at Big mound, in 1863, and some of the Western Indians at various points.

The Messengers to Sibley,

Wishing to get into communication with Little Crow, Sibley left a note on the battlefield at Birch Coulie, (See page 66). At a council of the hostiles it was decided to answer the message. Thomas A. Robertson tells the following story:

Tom Robinson, was one mixed-blood chosen to go, but no other was willing to chance a visit to the whites, after the outbreak. I told him I would go, if permitted. When he told Little Crow, he said: "No, find some one else." But he could not find any one. They were afraid. I had known Little Crow from childhood; I presume he did not want me to go as I was the head of the family. Then Tom and I went to Little Crow's tent, and as he saw me he said: "Tonska ya hi", (nephew, or relative, you have come—all Dakotas are relatives), and he told me to sit by him. Tom then told him that no other was willing to go, and that he did not want to go alone. He said: "Are you not afraid?" I told him I was not afraid to go anywhere he sent me. Then he said: "You two can go", and handed Tom the letter. We were then at Yellow Medicine about 35 miles from Ft. Ridgely. Tom told him it was a long walk and we would return soon as possible. He then told us we would not have to walk, and got us a small mule and a single buggy. This mule would lope all day, but could not trot. We started on our way and got a piece of cloth from an Indian grave near Yellow Medicine River, for a flag of truce. About a mile before we got to the fort we stopped and hid our guns. When we came in sight of the fort there was quite a commotion, and a man from the fort then came out to meet us. When near the picket line I got out and went to meet him. This man was Col. McPhail. He asked where we were from, and I told him from Little Crow with a message to Sibley. He then got in the buggy with us and taking the lines drove into the fort, while a detachment of troops guarded us on the way. We were conducted to Col. Sibley, and then given supper, and were afterward examined separately. We had agreed on our answers to main questions to be asked, so our statements tallied well. I bore a secret message from the friendly camp to Sibley, and successfully delivered it. The next morning early, an escort took us outside the lines, and we started

back, securing our guns on the way. We delivered
the answer to Little Crow. There was increasing
trouble between the two camps, and when we were
asked to go to Sibley again, I felt pretty squeamish.
Many hostiles would have shot me down, had they
known of the secret message. Wakinyan-waxte
(Good thunder), the night before we were to start
told me that the friendlies wanted to send a letter to
Sibley, and wanted me to write it for them. To
prevent discovery, I got down under a blanket with
a lighted candle and wrote the letter. He said to
sign Taopi, (Wounded man) and Wapaxa's names to
the letter. Going down was without incident. We
started back toward night, and in the dusk, a hawk
fluttering in the weeds gave us visions of being waylaid, and near the Birch Coulie battlefiled a horrible
stench from the decaying bodies of a hundred horses
gave a sensation far from pleasant, and never forgotten. We stayed over night at Beaver Falls, and
next morning met Onktomi-ska (White spider), and
a band of hostiles. We were uneasy lest they meant
mischief to us, but an equal number of our friends
soon came up and our fears were allayed.

When we reached camp, Little Crow was dancing and singing: "The British are coming to help us,
and are bringing Little Dakota". This was a small
cannon left by some early explorers near Jamestown,
N. D.; it was afterward thrown into the river. In a
few days word was brought in by runners, that Sibley's army was coming, and the bloody Cut Nose,

chief of the Soldier's Lodge, ordered all men to go to Wood Lake to fight. Fear of disobeying and desire to see the outcome took nearly everyone to the field, but many returned in the night, and the friendlies kept together, aside from the fighting. When the hostiles came back defeated and discouraged they found the friendlies had secured all the prisoners in their camp, had dug pits for protection, and were ready to meet the objectors on any grounds chosen. They had no time to argue, and by morning there were no hostiles—all had fled to the West.

MAZA-KUTE-MANI,

(Shoots at metal as he walks—called Little Paul.)

(As very few people have any idea of the Dakota language, the following story and translation is given. It is written and translated by Thos. A. Robertson of Veblen, S. D., who has been an interpreter many years. Vowels are given the European sound.)

Wicaste kin de homaksina hihan tanhan sdonwaya ga oran wanfiksi sdonwaya ya wicasta kin de wokik-suye kta iyecica e ito oran wanziksi omdake kta. Inkpaduta waxicun wicakte kin he ehan wasicun winyan yamni wayaka wicaryuzapi Mrs. Noble, Mrs. Marble ga Miss Gardner. Mrs. Noble he ipaksan iyuwigapi kin hen miniabotapi. Mrs. Marble he Si-harota cincu kici huwi ipi ga ahdipi tka. Miss Gard-ner Wakeyaska amica ga icu okipipi sni. Mazakute-mani huwi mde kta ce eya minisou kin heciya iyeya, hinar Wakeyaska yuha um ga amica esta Mazakutemani icu ya ahdi. Token un de tanyan

sdonwaye cin he detu. Wansi he Mazakutemani
kici i kin he Pejuhuta-zizi gapi. Kin ekta hdi ga
xunka wakan kin manipisni ya iyopta okabipi sni
keya, Ate ekta yemasi ga Mde Iena hihan hdipi
ecan en wai ga he tanhan amica wahdi.

Wakeyaska wicaste xica ga wokipi yeyas wowa-
unsida iyotan e iyotan da kin kokipi sni decen econ.
Mazakutemani wicasta ksi xica heca sni, ohini war-
bayena piiciya wicaxta owasin kodaye kta cin. Tka
hehan wowaste ga wowotanna en takuna koki pi sni.
Ai tancanyan oranyi cin 1862 en Mdewakantonwan
waxicun wicakte kin hentu Sissetonwan ga Warpetonwan kin hecetu sni dapi ga un meniciyapi Taoyateduta tona om najin om is eya omniciye kin he
en unpi ga om hdokinicapi. Taoyatedute, Sissetonwan ga Warpetonwan kin is eya waxicun kizapi ga
iye okiyapi kta kta hean cin ga he ohna wohdeke
tuka. Mazakutemani ayupte ca heya, tohini waxicun
wicayakte kin de cin acanu ga makoce kin den yaun
kta oya kihi sni. Hihan Taoyateduta is heya sag-
dasinta imdamde ga hiciya waun kta.

Mazakutemani is heya sagdasin itancan yuhapi
kin he winyan ga waunsida winyan ga hoksiyopa
unsikapi kin hena wicayakte ga teriya wicayakuwa
unkan tuwe hecan econ unkan he iciye ya iye en
wowinape iyeye kta okihe sni ya nakun ia pi ota un
waxicun iciye najin, ohnayan kokipi ga itonpi sni
eya, tka wowapi kin de amdake kta iyehantu sni,
e henana epe kta.

Translation—I have known this man since I was a

boy and known some of his acts, and as this man ought
to be remembered I will tell you of some of the things
that he did.   At the time Inkpaduta killed the whites,
three white women were taken prisoners—Mrs. Noble,
Mrs. Marble and Miss Gardner.   At the time they
crossed the Sioux River Mrs. Noble was shot to death
in the water.   Mrs. Marble was rescued by Siharota
(Gray foot) and his brother, but Mrs. Gardner, Wakeyaska (White lodge), would not give up, and they could
not take her.   Mazakutemani (Shoots at metal as he
walks) said, "I will go and get her"; he found her on
the Missouri river.   White lodge still had her, and
would not let her go, Mazakutemani took her and
brought her away.   The way I came to know this is,
there was another man that went with Mazakutemani
this man came to Yellow Medicine and said the horses
had played out, and could not go any further.

Father told me to go and get them, and I met them
at Lac qui Parle and brought them in from there.   Wakeyaska was a bad man and dangerous, but Mazakutemani did not fear him.   Mazakutemani was not a man
seeking trouble, he conducted himself peaceably and
wanted to be friendly with everybody, but in the cause
of right and justice he was afraid of nothing.   One of
his main acts was at the time the Medawakantons killed
the Whites in 1862; the Sissetons and Wapatons said it
was not right, and called a council.   Taoyateduta (Little Crow) and his followers were at that council and
had much talk.   Taoyateduta wanted the Sissetons and
Wapatons in the fighting of the Whites; but Mazakutemani said: "What you have done in the killing of the
Whites is such you can never stay in this country."
Then Taoyateduta said: "I will go to the English country, and stay there".   But Mazakutemani said: "The
Chief of the English is a woman, and kind; and what
you have done to the poor women and children—such a

man can never find protection from her". With many
more words he took the part of the Whites without fear
but in this paper I cannot tell all, so will close.

Sketch of Chief Little Crow.

Ta-oyate-duta, (His scarlet people), was the son
of Wakinyan-tanka, (Big thunder), a chief of the
Kaposia band, and his mother was Minni-oka-da-
win, (Empties into water).   He was born in 1820 and
became chief in 1846.   He was not a promising son,
but was a rover, and only by the death of two of
his brothers at the hands of the Objibwas, was he
named as chief.   His father, who was accidentally
mortally wounded, told him this, and that he should
seek advice from Sibley.   There was contention over
the appointment resulting in an affray, in which the
young chief was shot through both wrists, and two
brothers were killed.   The Medicine Men of the
band managed to save the arms, but the deformity
was a disgrace always concealed.   From this time
he showed great improvement so that he was prominent in the Treaty of 1851, and was one of those
who received the bribe money, some $3,000 each.
He had, before his appointment, married four daughters of a Wapaton chief, Iyang-mani, (Running
walker), but when he married the third one, he put
aside the first two.

In 1862 Little Crow was much in disfavor, as a
result of his acts, especially in connection with the

sale of a part of the reservation, or rather the settlement of a sale forced on the Indians by the government. Yet, when the crisis came he was first choice to lead the warpath. He was awakened from his slumbers by the Rice Creek band, who explained the Acton murders and demanded his support, which he finally gave. The failure to conquer either the fort or New Ulm, and his own disgust with the maudlin acts and condition of his warriors, aroused dissension so that he, with a chosen band went to the north on a marauding expedition. While absent the unsuccessful battle at Birch Coulie was fought. The note left by Sibley to Little Crow, put him in the position as the leader to be treated with. But he knew the end to come. His answer to Sibley was not a plea for peace, but rather a defiance. As the battle of Wood Lake came on, the situation was very discouraging. The Sibley forces were more than double any force he could muster, and of the 800 Indians at least a half were opposed or indifferent. Standing Buffalo told him to "Fight it out himself; and keep off the Sisseton reservation"; Red Iron had met him with force and compelled him to stop; Little Paul and the Wapaton Soldier's Lodge had grown strong enough to defy him, and Wapasha, Taopi and others had deserted to the friendly camp. Every direction was clouded with trouble and discouragment, and the frantic efforts by the hostiles brought out only 738 warriors, including many boys; many went who had no intention of fighting. After the battle all was confusion; one infuriated father tried to shoot Little Crow to avenge the death of a son; all the captives were in the friendly camp. which was prepared for battle. He gathered his followers and left for the western wilds. He was a "down and out" and a miserable failure—his chieftanship was buried in ignominy and disgrace.

He was avoided and warned off by the Sissetons, attacked by the western tribes, refused shelter by the British authorities, and finally shot down by a farmer and son, while on a trip to steal horses to enable him to hunt buffalo. Indians to show their defiance for their enemies committed many atrocities; in like manner the Whites mutilated his body, and kept his scalp, for which a reward was paid, on exhibition for more than 50 years. From an Indian view Little Crow was the consistent leader of a lost cause, for which he gave his life and all he possessed. He has been pictured as the demon of the massacre so persistently that the real barbarians have been forgotten. There is no evidence that Little Crow ever killed a white person, and it is true that he saved the lives of at least several prisoners, at great personal danger. Few know of Cut Nose, Inkpaduta, Striped Arrow, inhuman brutes and many times over murderes. but the historians have branded him so long as the memory lasts.

The mortality record of his family is: Father killed by accident, two brothers by Objibways, two in tribal quarrel, two sisters by suicide.

INTERESTING NOTES.

JOHN OTHERDAY PARTY.

The Upper Agency employes, and residents under guidance of Otherday, fled on Tuesday morning, August 19th, and finally arrived at Hutchinson. If there is any list of the 62 persons composing the party, it has not been made public.

THE MISSIONARY PARTY.

The S. R. Riggs and Thomas S. Williamson Missions were located near the Upper Agency. Monday evening the 18th; friendly Indians warned these and their white friends to flee as they could not protect them. Riggs and party were conducted to an island, and the next morning united with the Williamson party except Williamson and wife, started to the northeast across the prairie. When they struck the Lac qui Parle trail they went toward Ft. Ridgley. Finding it improbable that they would succeed in entering the fort they took course toward Henderson which point they reached on Mondy the 25th. In this party were Riggs and family, Williamson's (including the Doctor and wife who overtook them), Miss Jane, sister to Williamson, H. D. Cunningham and family, Andrew Hunter, son-in-law of Williamson, and wife, D. W. Moore and wife, Jonas Pettijohn and family, Sophie Robertson, Adrian J. Ebell, Richard Orr, a wounded fugitive, one Gilligan and

three Germans. These latter five men overtook and
joined the party. When near New Ulm Gilligan and
the Germans left the party for that town and were
killed. A picture of this party was taken when near
present Bird Island, by Ebell. In the copies found
some artist has added flavor by introducing John
Otherday in the group. This has caused many to
believe it the Otherday party.

THE SCALP DANCE.

Thomas A. Robertson, describes the scalp dance
and capture as follows:

The scalps were stretched on hoops, dried, and
painted red on the flesh side, and the hair decorated
with ribbons, feathers, etc. The scalps were kept
for four months, and at each new moon, were re-
painted, re-decorated, and a feast and grand dance
was held, which sometimes lasted several days, then
a grave was dug and the scalp buried. These month-
ly renewings of the scalp, were called: "The painting
of the scalps," by the Dakotas. From the time of
taking of the scalp to the time of burial of the same
the one taking the scalp and three others (if connect-
ed with the taking), were not allowed to use any
flashy paint, or personal decorations of any kind,
except to wear on top of his head, a tuft of swan's
down about the size of an apple. His blanket, usually an old one, daubed with mud, and his face painted
black. The one who did the actual killing is given a
separate honor—then comes the "coups", which are
the touching of the enemy's body, apparently dead,

or lying near the enemies. Of these there are four on the body of each enemy killed, and it is deemed more of an honor than the actual killing. In some cases the man who did the killing would make the first "coup", and if so, he is accorded a double honor, which was the wearing of an eagle feather, on the white part of which was painted a red spot, Only three more "coups" could be taken on that body. Each person was allowed to wear one eagle feather for each "coup" performed.

FORTS AND BLOCK HOUSES.

In a few days after it was found that the outbreak was a certainty. citizens at many points prepared to defend themselves and property. Stockades were erected at Hutchinson, where the park is now, at Forest City, Corinna twp. (now Annandale), Fair Haven and Clearwater; at St. Cloud Broker's brick building was fortified, and a stockade was put up on the brow of a hill in the lower town. Only the first two were attacked. Several of these were made of two rows of logs on end, overlapping, and with corner towers set out to prevent approach at the sides. A well and cellar were dug inside, and fuel and ammunition stored. The State issued muskets (made in 1818 in Austria), which carried an ounce ball, and with black powder made noise enough to scare off evil spirits and "kicked" as viciously as an army mule. These guns were not in favor with the marksmen, and they refused to give up their long-barrelled hunting rifles for them.

NEW ULM CASUALTIES.

The victims of the battle at New Ulm numbered 26, which was not equalled in any other fight during the outbreak, and this despite barracks. Possibly the terror of the overcrowded town by those who witnessed bloody scenes, helped. The muskets captured, by the Indians at the ferry battle may have been a factor. The following were killed:

Ahearn, Matthew	Barth, G. W. Otto
Buggert, Otto	Castor, Jacob
Dodd, William B.	Edwards, A. W.
England, William	Haack, Max
Haberle, Jacob	Houghton, Newell E.
Huggins, Rufus	Kirchstein, Julius
Krause, Ferdinand	Krieger, John, Sr.
Kulp, Washington	Lusky, William
Maloney, William	Meyer, Matthias
Michaels, John C.	Nicholson, William
Quane, Jerry	Rieman, August
Roepke, August	Senzke, Leopold
Somers, John	Smith, Luke

This list does not include the people killed on Tuesday previous. Of the 51 killed in Milford, the greater part were related in the town, and those who escaped brought the tales of horror most vividly to the frightened people. Plans were laid for self-destruction of the women, if the town was captured. One man died of fright, one attempted to leave the town and was killed, one half-crazed man was trying to burn the town. It was indeed due to the cool management of Col. Flandreau that a panic was prevented which would have meant annihilation.

Anson Northrup's Mounted Volunteers.

(Note — The following Company roll was used at the 30th Anniversary Re-union, held at the West Hotel, Minneapolis, on August 22d, 1892. The copy is owned *by* Harris P., a son of Alvin Stone, a member of the company.)

When the news of the outbreak reached St. Anthony and Minneapolis there was a desire on the part of the citizens to know just how much there was in the terrifying reports. Under Anson Northrup, an experienced frontiersman. proprietor of the St. Charles Hotel in St. Anthony, this company was organized. Each member provided his own mount and arms, which comprised driving and work horses, rifles, shot-guns, muskets, etc. R. H. Chittenden of the 1st Wis. Cavalry was the drill-master. It was a very impromptu affair, and lumbermen, merchants professionals and tradesmen filled up the ranks. At St. Peter the company joined with some regular troops under Col. McPhail, and all made an all-night ride, reaching Fort Ridgely in the early morning of the 27th. Finding that the Indians had failed to capture either the fort or New Ulm, and had gone some 30 miles up the Minnesota river, they determined to return home. The military authorities tried to hold them and matters were hot for a time. They were roundly denounced and ridiculed long after to their annoyance and disgust. Two members joined the military; J. W. DeCamp whose home was

at the Lower Agency, and whose family were prisoners among the Indians, joined and was killed at
the Birch Coulie battle, Sept. 2d.   The family were
assisted to escape by Towan-ite-ta-ton (Face of the
village), and arrived at the fort, there to learn of the
husband and father's death.   Joseph Kellene also
enlisted and was mortally wounded at the same battle.   He was buried in the Maple Hill cemetery and
his grave was one of those obliterated by the un-
grateful City of Minneapolis, to make a park, and
his name is mangled in official records.   Such is the
private soldier's reward and glory.

NORTHRUP'S MOUNTED VOLUNTEERS

Capt.—Anson Northrup.
1st Lieut —Simon P. Snyder.
2d Lieut.—Edward Patch.
Drill-master—R. H. Chittenden.

Bassett, Daniel
Blaisdell, William
     ”   Robert
Barnard, Albion
     ”   John F.
Barker, Anson
Bowdish, S. S.
Brown, Baldwin
Bartholomew, R. H.
Bugbee, Riley
Berkman, E. C.
Chamberlain, W. H.
Crawford, Charles
Clark, Perry B.
Cahill, W. F.
Chase, W. H. H.

Jones, Steven H.
Jameson, John
Kent, A. E.
King, O. B.
Kellene, Joseph
Ladd, Joseph W.
Lambert, Edson
Lane, Silas
Lucas Charles
Laramie, Louis
Libby, A. D.
Moriarity, Thomas
McAbe, M. M.
Miner, N. H.
McMullen, James
McHerron, James

Covell, Marcus
Day, Daniel
    "   Horatio
    "   Gancelo
Dugan, Wm. M.
Dunbar, Owen
DeCamp, J. W.
Downs, Zelotes
Edwards, Newton
Eastman, John W.
Erwin, Everett
Farnham, S. W.
Freniere, Antoine
Fraker, Phillip
Gardiner, Thomas
Groff, Edward A.
    "   Al.
Gray, Thomas K.
Hanson, Gilbert
Hopper, Henry
Hunt, J. W.
Hayes, Moses P.
    "   E.
Hepp, Charles
Harmon, Chandler
Hawkes, ———
Hechtman, Henry

Nash, Edgar
Neudeck, A.
Pomeroy. J. W.
Quinn, William
Ryan, Patrick
Rogers, Orin
Redfield, David
Roach, P. K.
Rye, Charles
Rollins, Daniel
    "   M. B.
Stinson, William
Stone, Alvin
    "   H. W.
Shaw, Sidney
Stetson, Isaac G.
Smith, R. R.
Thompson, J. H.
Turner, S. W.
Upton, Charles
Vail, Geo. T.
VanAlstine, V. N.
Wells, Geo. G.
Wiggins, J. W.
Wilson, Horace
Young, John S.
Ainsworth, William

Townsend, Den.

Massacre Chronological Record.

Aug. 17—Murders at Acton.

Aug. 18—Outbreak at Lower Agency; massacres there also at Milford, LaCroix Creek, Beaver Creek, Middle Creek. Ambush at the Ferry.

Aug. 19—Massacre at Sacred Heart Creek, and at Upper Agency; massacre of Rescue party and attack on New Ulm.

Aug. 20—Massacre at Lake Shetek, and in Kandiyohi Counties; attack on Fort Ridgely.

Aug. 23—Battle at New Ulm.

Sept. 2—Battle at Birch Coulie.

Sept. 2-3-4—Battles at Forest City—Acton—and Hutchinson.

Sept. 23—Battle at Wood Lake.

Sept. 26—Surrender at Camp Release.

Dec. 26—Hanging at Mankato.

June '63—Condemned shipped to Davenport, Iowa, and tribes to Crow Creek, Dak. Ter.

1863-4-5—Sibley campaign, various murders, John Campbell hung near Mankato, Shapki and Medicine Bottle at Fort snelling,

Citizens killed or died from injuries.	413
Enlisted Soldiers,	77
Total killed,	490
Indians killed, hung or died,	71
Imprisoned,	277

LIST OF PERSONS KILLED.

(For 77 Enlisted soldier victims see State records,)

Austin, Andrew	60	Cross, Daniel	57
Anderson, Mary	43	Davis, Thos. J.	59
Adams, infant	57	Davies, LeGrande	42
Armstrong, John	59	Deck, Phillip	57
Apfelbaum brothers,	45	DeCamp, J. W.	65
Axe, Johannes	58	Dickinson, Lathrop	15
Backlund. Sven H.	56	" J. C.	65
Baker, Howard	11	Divoll, Geo. W.	14
Battins, Charles	61	Diederich, A.	40
Bennett, James	60	Drexler, Benedict	42
Belland, Joseph	15	Duley, Wm. children	54
Belzer, ——	42	Dubuque, Alexis	49
Boelter, Gottlieb, f'm.	29	Dustin, family	60
Boelter, John, family	29	Eastlick, family	51-54
Boelter, Michael, fam.	28	Earle, Radnor	24
Bosche, Henry	59	Ellingson, Gabriel	59
Busse, Gottfried fam.	30	Edwards, James	59
Bluem, family	43	Eisenreich, Balthasar	26
Broberg, Dan'l, family	55	Endreson, Lars	55
Broberg, Ander, family	55	Endreson, Endre	56
Broberg, Johannes	55	Evans, ——	61
Brown, family	44	Everett, Wm. family	51
Brook, Thomas	37	Foot, Silas	61
Buehro, John	38	Fehrenbach, Martin	61
Blair, Charles	86	Frass, John	27
Carrothers. children	24	" August family	33
Carroll, Wm. B.	46	"Fritz"	15
Carlson, Carl J.	56	Fohre, Ole	58
Cant, A. S.	58	Fink, family	42
Constans, Louis	49	Fenske, Jullus	40
Clausen, Frederick	37	Gleason, Geo. H.	48
Clausen, Charles	37	Gluth, John	42

Omitted by error: Robt. Jones, of Cambria; Therese Eggenhofer of Milford; Christian Richter of Courtland; Joseph Brosseau at Lower Agency; Andrew Bahlke of Birch Coulie.

Index of Events.